Translation Excellence:
Assessment
Achievement
Maintenance

AMERICAN TRANSLATORS ASSOCIATION
SCHOLARLY MONOGRAPH *Series*

Volume I   1987

EDITED BY

Marilyn Gaddis Rose

University Center at Binghamton (SUNY)

Printed in the United States of America

The American Translators Association *Series* is a hardcover monograph published periodically at the University Center at Binghamton (SUNY) by the Translation Research and Instruction Program. Since contributions are solicited by the Editors, prospective contributors are urged to query the Managing Editor or the Topic Editor before submission. The submission deadline for the 1988 volume "Technology as Translation Strategy" is February 1, 1987; the editor is Muriel Vasconcelos (Pan American Health Organization), 1802 Corcoran Street, N.W., Washington, D.C. 20009. The submission deadline for the 1989 volume "Translator Training and Foreign Language Pedagogy" is February 1, 1988; the editor is Peter W. Krawutschke (Western Michigan University), Translation Center, Languages and Linguistics, WMU, Kalamazoo, Michigan 49008.

Managing Editor: Marilyn Gaddis Rose,
Translation Research & Instruction Program
University Center at Binghamton (SUNY)
Binghamton, New York 13901 USA

Editorial Advisory Board: Ted Crump, National Institutes of Health Library (Bethesda, Maryland); Peter W. Krawutschke, Western Michigan University (Kalamazoo); Mildred L. Larson, Summer Institute of Linguistics (Dallas, Texas); Sue Ellen Wright, Linguistic Information Specialists, Inc. (Berea, Ohio)
Editorial Staff: Gabriela Mahn, Alice Otis, Michele J. Stern
Constituted as *Series* Subcommittee under the ATA Publications Committee, Ben Teague, chair.

Individuals (prepaid only):
☐ 1 vol. $15.
☐ 2 vols. $28.
☐ 3 vols. $39.

Institutions (prepaid or billed):
☐ 1 vol. $20.
☐ 2 vols. $40.
☐ 3 vols. $60.

Make checks, money order, or purchase order to:
ATA *Series*, TRIP, SUNY-Binghamton
Binghamton, NY 13901 USA

Subscribers outside the U.S. and its possessions are requested to make check payable to an American bank in U.S. dollars.

American Translators Association *Series*

TRANSLATION EXCELLENCE: ASSESSMENT, ACHIEVEMENT, MAINTENANCE

Volume I   1987

Contents

Editor's Note: What Translation Excellence Entails

MARILYN GADDIS ROSE

As quality and concept, excellence in translation is multidimensional and all-encompassing. Excellence in translation suggests first appropriate or adequate rendering of a source language text for a target language audience. "Appropriate" or "adequate" here means suitable both for the text in question and suitable for the audience. "Appropriate" and "adequate" can imply – and usually do – accuracy, completeness, felicity. All contributors assume these last attributes, whatever aspect of translation they address. Second, excellence suggests achieving and maintaining high standards like accuracy, completeness, felicity, for the tasks carried out by language specialists require training through supervised experience and/or formal education, continuing professional growth, and peer monitoring and verification. Third, each component of achievement and maintenance has standards and certification stages of its own. The profession, long overdue in being recognized as a profession in the United States, has a stake in postsecondary and continuing education, the status and working conditions of translators, their recruitment and retention, and, above all, their qualifications for being in the profession. For this reason, the profession, represented here by the American Translators Association, has viewed credentialing translators and establishing ethical working guidelines as practical matters, which are vital for standards and hence, factors in excellence.

Traditionally, translators work alone or in small teams. Dictionaries and writing machines are their steady companions, and their only interpersonal encounters in the course of a long work day may be with casual acquaintances in a research library staff or voices recorded on their answering machines – or even more impersonal terminology messages from their data banks. Yet they are committed to pleasing the user by producing target-language texts that will be excellent by their clients' criteria and their own. Translators worry, for they know that such excellent products are not always readily achieved on one's own. There is the harassment of inadequate time, the anxiety of unavailable information, the betrayal of deficient references, the ever-lurking writer's block which may sometimes be especially acute for translators since they must retrieve two or more languages from the store in their own minds.

Paradoxically perhaps, while translators, inevitably individualists, may not agree on discrete choices in discrete texts, they are united on excellence. They recognize it, probably more quickly than the average educated reader since they could not translate at all if they did not continually internalize the changing style norms of the target language. They agree upon it. The difficulty lies not in defining excellence but in achieving and maintaining it. As a group of professionals, they are concerned with protecting standards, developing safeguards ensuring such protection, and, to a lesser extent, educating the translation user and the public at large on the requisite conditions for translation excellence.

Translators proceed always from a concept of the ideal, flawless translation, a concept which may seem mystical to outsiders. The parameters and surface of the ideal are relative, but the concept is absolute. Anna Lilova, president of the Fédération Internationale des Traducteurs with which the ATA is affiliated, and György Radó, editor-in-chief of the FIT journal *Babel*, discuss such a concept in their essays welcoming the ATA *Series* into the worldwide library of FIT publications. Since Madame Lilova is a Bulgarian who submitted her essay in French, and Dr. Radó is a Hungarian who does not usually write in English, their essays here are, additionally, proof that translation not only conveys information but eloquence and persuasion also.

The ATA founders, as the essays of ATA President Patricia E. Newman and past President Ben Teague emphasize, were dedicated from the outset to developing ways to identify competent translators and providing access to continuing education. In the subsequent quarter century of ATA activity, fewer translators have become translators through happenstance, and more language professionals have become translators through special training.

This has meant that the ATA has looked to Academia, and, reciprocally, the translators in Academia have looked to the ATA. As long as there was—or was felt to be—a balance between supply and demand, there was little mutual pressure to bring translators and postsecondary education into the same kind of relationship as that between schools and lawyers, physicians, engineers, etc. The balance has been changing, and mutual pressures now exist. Richard Brod and Peter W. Krawutschke take up the issues and strategies proposed to ensure standards among degree-granting institutions.

It is at this juncture that the *Series* staff has asked foreign-language proficiency experts to consider the applicability of their testing procedures to translation so that performance expected in the workplace can be predicted from performance in the classroom. The feasibility is explored in the symposium article which Gabriela Mahn has organized with Jerry W. Larson, James R. Child, Pardee Lowe, Jr., and Martha Herzog.

Series also called on a major world translation and translator training institution the Summer Institute of Linguistics for a summation of its criteria for determining translation acceptability. This is the essay of Mildred L. Larson.

The procedures for recruitment and retention at the United Nations which works under awesome pressure to convey accuracy and style, even emotional nuance, are outlined by Françoise Cestac, UN Translation Director; those of an international agency are itemized by Eric Norman McMillan, while Alice Otis and Ted Crump and Timothy Rowe take up safeguards for standards in national agencies.

Government and Academia, however, have numerous personnel and, relatively, greater material resources to deploy in their operations. It is the symposium article organized by Sue Ellen Wright which actually deals with the traditional translator intent upon the same high standards but often with fewer resources and less time. Her colleagues from the principal areas of private-sector translating—S. Edmund Berger, Doris Ganser, Kurt Gingold, and Josephine Thornton—define their terms and explain their strategies for matching translation to client.

But while human lives, national economies, and international relations depend upon the work of these translators, usually anonymous, their clients exercise responsibility for audience welfare. This is different, at least in degree, from the literary translator, who even more than the non-literary translator, works in isolation for readers who may pick up the translation and be affected by it as long as the target language survives. Peter Glassgold and Michael Scott Doyle with Anthony Kerrigan take up that charge. It is well they do, for they bring us back to the exhilaration and satisfaction of translating. Counterpointing the harassment of inadequate time is the luxuriance of the leisurely revision. Counterpointing the anxiety of unavailable information and the betrayal of deficient references is the joy of the multitude of facts and insights gained along the way to that elusive term – facts and insights which in time will serve. Even the most specialized translators become Renaissance persons. Counterpointing the ever-lurking writer's block is the serendipity of the perfect match and the convincing analogue. Even isolation has its counterpoint: one enters the mind of an area expert or tries out the personality of a literary genius, and when translators work with living authors, they usually add them to their store of friendships. Finally, there is the deep satisfaction of having provided a service indispensable to humanity and human history.

Human beings need translation for survival: for sharing information daily, recording and enriching over time. In translation, excellence is comprehensive and vital.

* * * * * * * *

We acknowledge with thanks the gracious permissions extended by the following publishers: for quotations from Eleanor Shipley Duckett, *Alfred the Great: the King and His England* (1956) printed with the kind permission of the University of Chicago Press which holds the copyright; Paul Auster, editor, *The Random House Book of Twentieth-Century French Poetry* (1982) and James Joyce, *Ulysses* (1961 edition), printed with the kind permission of Random House, Inc. which holds the copyrights; Alan Duff, *The Third Language: Recurrent Problems of Translation into English* (1981) and Peter Newmark, *Approaches to Translation* (1981) to Pergamon Press which holds the copyrights.

American Translators Association *Series*

TRANSLATION EXCELLENCE: ASSESSMENT, ACHIEVEMENT, MAINTENANCE

Volume I   1987

ATA's Commitment to Excellence

PATRICIA E. NEWMAN

When the American Translators Association was founded in 1959, its certificate of incorporation listed the purposes for which the corporation was formed:

a) To advocate and promote the recognition of translation as a profession.

b) To formulate and maintain standards of professional ethics, practices, and competence.

c) To improve the standards, quality, and rewards of translation.

The certificate goes on to list seven more purposes, but these first three are enough to demonstrate that the ATA has felt a commitment to excellence from its very beginning.

The ATA includes all three members of the translation profession: freelance translators, in-house translators, and translation companies. It may be thought that the interests of translation companies and freelance translators conflict, but in fact they do not. After all, translation companies have just as much interest in translation excellence and the recognition of translation as a profession as do freelance translators. By including companies among its members, the ATA expands the recognition and endorsement of its code of ethical practices and enlists a powerful ally in its battle for professional recognition.

Excellence in translation is not just consistent, competent performance on the job, although that is its cornerstone. Excellence encompasses ethical behavior, a commitment to continuing education, and fulfillment of professional obligations.

It is common to think of ethics as primarily a matter of financial dealings: how much and how promptly a translation company pays a translator, whether a freelance undercuts a colleague or cheats a subcontractor, whether a client pays the full amount on time. However, ethics extends to many other facets of the profession. Is it ethical to accept a job for which one is unqualified? To accept an impossible deadline, knowing it won't be met? To advertise skills or certification one does not have? To do a mediocre job for a client who can't tell the difference? All of these questions lie within the realm of ethical behavior, and they all pertain to standards of excellence. The ATA's Ethics Committee works constantly to guide its members through the thickets of ethical practice.

Excellence is founded on the cornerstone of competent, consistent performance. A moment's reflection is enough to show that performance over a long period of time cannot be maintained on the knowledge one brings to the profession as a beginner. Science and technology, for example, are advancing at an exponential rate, and a translator must keep up with new developments or risk becoming as obsolete as the abacus in an engineering laboratory. Even the skills of the profession, whether writing or interpreting, become dull over the years unless honed under the guidance of a respected teacher. Continuing education is the answer to this problem.

If consistent, competent performance and ethical practice are two legs of the tripod of professional excellence, the third must be the fulfillment of professional obligations. "Professionals" were defined at the 25th anniversary conference of the ATA as follows.

1. Professionals bring a background of scholarship to their work. This implies formal, higher education.
2. Professionals practice sound craftsmanship and consistently produce work of good quality and professional merit.
3. Professionals hold high standards of ethical conduct in the face of daily temptation.

4. Professionals resist demeaning working conditions, substandard pay, and low public opinion.
5. Professionals participate in the professional community.
6. Professionals, recognizing their obligation to the novice, teach the apprentices who will follow them in order that the profession not fall into disgrace.
7. Professionals write for publication, not just to share their knowledge with others, but also because writing exercises the scholarship they worked to achieve and provides the self-discipline they need to hone the skills of communication that are essential to this profession.

This definition of "professional" applies equally well to excellence. An excellent translator is a professional.

The ATA supports its members as they strive for excellence by supporting all of these component parts. Its Translation Studies Committee works with academic institutions to recognize and encourage outstanding training programs for translation and interpretation. Its most recent publication is the 1983 *Survey of Schools and Institutions Offering Translator and Interpreter Training*. The Continuing Education Committee sponsors workshops and seminars at the annual conference and at other times and places throughout the year to enable ATA members to hone their professional skills. Eight ATA chapters offer year-round opportunities for participation in the professional community through meetings and the publication of newsletters, while the annual ATA conference provides unparalleled opportunities for making professional contacts, learning new concepts, and becoming acquainted with new tools.

Perhaps the major ATA achievement in support of professional excellence is the accreditation program, in which candidates attempt to demonstrate sound craftsmanship by writing proctored examinations in any one of 14 language pairs. Those who meet certain minimum standards are granted accreditation in the specific language pair. This program will soon be supplemented by ATACERT, which will grant the title of Fellow to those who pass its rigorous examination standards in a particular language pair and subject specialty.

Publications are a good indicator of a professional association's commitment to excellence, and the ATA now offers four regular publications. The ATA *Chronicle*, a monthly newsletter, has been published under various titles since the inception of the organization in 1959. *Proceedings* of the annual conference have been published since the 25th anniversary in 1984, and the *Translation Services Directory*, a listing of accredited members with their backgrounds, language and subject specialties, and accreditation records, is now in its sixth edition. The newest component of the publication program is this journal, a thematic annual which will provide a forum for scholarly papers that are not appropriate for a newsletter.

All of this activity in support of excellence in translation is the more remarkable when one considers that it is based on volunteer effort. Officers, directors, and committee heads work without pay, and the countless hours that each contributes are convincing evidence that the ATA and its individual members are strongly committed to excellence in translation.

The Perfect Translation — Ideal and Reality

ANNA LILOVA

The problem of perfect translation is as old as translation itself. Evident since the very beginning of the practice of this activity, it is as natural as it is inevitable:

— as an attempt by society, and by readers in particular, to identify the perfect translation,
— as an attempt of the very art of translation, to outline itself, to define itself at the heart of translation science, as an ideal, as a special and independent activity.

In the millenial history of translation, every given period has sought a solution to this problem, ideal in solution, real in resolution.

There were periods where *word-for-word* was considered ideal translation, the word being considered not as a formal linguistic unit, but as an independent semantic unit; the first translations of religious texts provide supporting evidence. The explanation is simple; divine word and expression are sacred. This translation technique may very well seem mechanical and oversimplified, but on the other hand it expresses totality of comprehension and reproduction, the first transparency between languages, to such an extent that word-for-word can be designated as the coinciding of literal and free translation, and be considered in certain respects as the first representation of the ideal in translation. A certain difference exists between the word-for-word of a manual done by Cicero, considered more like a glossary, and the word-for-word translations starting with Greek, done by the creators of the Slavic alphabet and the first translators, the Constantine brothers Cyril the philosopher and Methodius. This difference lies in the consideration of the syntactical peculiarities of the target language. Translating from an advanced language, they accomplished the considerable task of enriching and improving a national language, furnishing the Slavic people with a new spiritual material. Moreover, their translations, which had a universal cultural value, played a mediating role between the Byzantine culture and the cultures of the Slavs of the east and south.

Still during other periods, *literal translation* meant perfect translation. The latter, needless to say, goes beyond the meaning of different elements, their function, and their connection with the sum total. In its historical aspect, it brings forth the absolute, obvious, unique, isolated, and specific to draw the literal into translation. In other words, veracity in translation signifies a mechanical transposition of the unique, of the elements of form ignoring their functions, not heeding their links with the sum total. This formal approach of equivalence between original and translation has, during given historic periods, determined the character and the quality of translations in the framework of a national literature. Literal translation disparages translation overall, alienates it from the original, even more so in the case of literary works.

Yet during certain periods, *free translation* was the ideal of perfect translation. The example "des belles infidèles" may be cited, typical of Western literatures and especially of France in the XVIIth and XVIIIth centuries at the time of absolutism, Germany of the XVth century, Russia at the end of the XVIIIth century and the beginning of the XIXth century. Free translation is characterized by emphasizing the general nature, the general idea in a given work, i.e., veracity is identified with ignoring the individual in the original in the name of a *grosso modo* coincidence between the original and the translation. Free translation allowed for the subjective interference and the "embellishment" of the original in good faith, while ignoring linguistic and stylistic specifics.

Still from a historical perspective, it is necessary to mention hesitancies as far as perfect translation is concerned, from the time of Goethe and Schleiermacher: whether it benefits the translation, or it benefits the original. Both tendencies were defended in the name of faithful translation. Nevertheless, it is evident that the ideal balance between word-for-word, and literal and free in the framework of the original and the translation cannot be reached. In the first case a Germanization of the translated text takes place (the translations of the German reformer

Martin Luther), i.e., a localization and actualization in the target language of elements specific to the original; in the second case, the accent is placed on the source language, from which the translation is "alienated," defended, and achieved in practice by Schleiermacher in his translations of Plato's works. This artificial opposition between original and translation can only be explained in a well-defined social context.

But beyond these extreme considerations of the perfect translation, the dimensions and facets of which are different from one national literature to another, a principle has existed along with the evolution of translation, a principle which little by little has taken over — that of recreating the original in an adequate way, through the means of the target language, taking into consideration the general and the specific, the substance and the form, the unique and the common — the principle of the *adequate translation*. This concept was initially limited to literary translation and began with the theoretical arguments of Cicero about the coincidence of *res et verba*. The evolution of other genres of translation (scientific, documentary) made this demand extend its parameters and specified its content. Adequate translation comes closest to the qualities of the original in the context of its new linguistic existence.

It is evident that leaning towards one ideal or another when it comes to perfect translation, the affirmation of one principle or another in the framework of national cultures and of universal culture is not an accident. These phenomena follow from numerous factors which influenced one another, influencing the very process of translation. The motivations here are diverse, the most important ones being dictated by the needs of given national cultures. Each national cultural history demonstrates many conflicting tendencies and manners of rendering a text which exist concurrently and follow each other, resulting in the conflicts and changes occuring within various literary trends and domination of some given genre. However, they always meet the spiritual needs of a given national culture.

The different types of translation are intimately linked to one another. We cannot restrict ourselves to the statement that translations of Shakespeare into Russian during the 1820's came closest to the original, without mentioning that it was really Shakespeare, his ideas, and his magnificent characters which at that particular time required translation as close to the original as possible. This type of translation had already replaced the preceding ideal of "embellished" translation because this new concept had already appeared in the context of Romanticism, modeling the image of Russian literature in the early 1820's.

And if it is permitted to speak of *progress* in the concept of perfect translation, this progress is above all applied to the perception of the translated book by the reader and by society; this progress ascribes new dimensions to the ideal, owing to the ever more important abilities of deeper accession, in a polyphonic way, into the works of different authors, of different periods, of different peoples and cultures.

Starting with scholasticism, with its rules and dogmas, translation in the Middle Ages facilitated by its harshness and lack of flexibility not only the act of translation (word-for-word and literal translation were reduced to the substitution of linguistic elements) but the perception of the original as well. It may be easily affirmed that literal translation was known to "diminish" and "freeze" the potential value of the original. We need only remember the dogmatic sacred translations, which for thousands of years deprived world literature of the true beauty and real value of the Song of Solomon.

It may be contrarily confirmed that the ever-growing range of acceptance by the reader and the more professional interest brought into translation make free translation, despite "transgressions" vis-à-vis the original, a statement about the individual — about the personality of the translator; this idea is encouraged by the idea or illusion of more fully rendering the literary content of the original. One has only to cite the example of free translation of the XVIIIth century, obeying all the aesthetic norms of Classicism, characterized by mimicry and arbitrary adaptation of the original; its existence demonstrates that readers themselves sufficiently showed natural ability and flexibility with regard to a reproductive co-creation, giving proof of the free style and adaptation with regard to the ideal of prefigured beauty offered by the translated text.

Despite differences in the degree of cultural evolution of different countries and regions, of methods and phenomena of original literature, our period has and shapes a clear idea, a clear ideal of perfect translation. This ideal includes the specificities of different national cultures, taking into account the objectives of translation for their evolution, for the evolution of world culture.

Thus the image offered by culture today is greatly varied, as much from a national and social point of view as from a regional one. Each country gives clear content to the ideal, imposing its demands and needs, allowing for the needs of its own national culture and its own interpretation of the world cultural process.

But from the perspective of a synthesis of historical heritage, the essential demand of our time, the role of translation and the goal of the translator in the contemporary world, it is possible to outline, however relatively, the fundamental contours of the contemporary ideal of perfect translation. They could be defined in the following manner:

First: A perfect translation is a *necessary* translation. Necessary for:

—overall evolution of national culture;
—consideration of the given time and specific demands of this evolution;
—consideration of the very content of the original, its implication;
—consideration of the given reader, of his social and professional interests;
—the consideration of the demands of a given society.

Therefore, the most perfect translation from the professional point of view is ineffectual outside the context of the social and cultural demands which give it life.

It is evident that translated literature is not a phenomenon in and of itself, but an important factor, an integral part of the evolution of national cultures. Translation is a specific historical phenomenon, dictated by clear reasons, possessing its own means of development. It is born from social context, not resulting uniquely from subjective desires and interests; it is innate in the evolution of every nation. Born from society, translated literature returns to it making an impact, satisfying the needs of individuals and society. In and of itself, separated and isolated from the cultural and social processes, translation can neither appear, nor exist, nor evolve. Translation and the ideal of translation differ, as do the criteria of its evaluation from the Middle Ages to the Renaissance and our time.

With time, the amplitude, appreciation, and attitudes vis-à-vis the works of the past change. The attitude of the troubadour, author and interpreter of a knight's song, listener and reader of *Chanson de Roland* and ours vis-à-vis this same work are very different. The problems presented by the social critique of one of Jean-Jacques Rousseau's novels have a different impact on contemporary readers, in terms of the actual social situation, from that exercised on the readers living at the same time as Rousseau and in his society.

Second: A perfect translation is an *adequate* translation, which preserves and transposes the impact, meaning, ideas, beauty, and the entire value of the original into a new linguistic context. The ideal should be a multilateral adequacy, poly-adequacy. The objective: to transpose into the translation the whole texture of the original.

Adequacy of translation is historically conditioned. As a principle, it can be neither absolute nor unalterable. The image of Don Quixote in the Middle Ages is not and cannot be the same as it is today. For true equivalence, time plays a considerable role. Translation must take into account not only the historical authenticity of the original, but also the actual impact of the original. The translator must render Don Quixote as he was depicted by Cervantes in the XVIIth century, while presenting to the contemporary reader a Don Quixote who has not just come out of the museum, but who expresses the problems of today's man, who is an image of contemporary translation. This means real equivalence in translation must be at the same time faithful to the original, conceived vis-à-vis the moment of creation and the moment of translation.

Considered in this way, the principle of true equivalence, of adequate translation excludes free translation which is harmful to fidelity vis-à-vis the original, the period, and the author. Literal translation is also totally inadmissible because it "mummifies" the original text and destroys the meaning, breaking the connection of the original with reality. Translation is not the preservation of the original, but a continuation in another time, for other generations, in another social milieu. Therefore, such translation is the supreme synthesis of the historical and contemporary existence of the original.

The different types of translation, word-for-word, literal translation, and free translation, have prepared and shown the way for formation of equivalent translation which must on the one hand faithfully render the true and total complexity of the original, and on the other hand safeguard the qualitative characteristics in aiming for the most perfect and natural equilibrium between the original and the translation. E. A. Nida observed at the 1977 FIT Congress in Montreal that translation, strictly rendered, cannot be equivalent in a dynamic way because it is deprived of the possibility of being a natural equivalent to the original text. Thanks to the principle of dynamic equivalence in the translation process, Nida on the one hand aims for the communicative effect of the message, communication in the sense of "dynamic interpretation," and on the other hand for a balance of effect between original and translation while preserving fidelity vis-à-vis the language, the original text, and the readers.

Translation is considered a complex activity, multilateral as well as total, as a specific system – structured and functioning, a system where all the elements are linked to one another, interdependent and interacting. This interaction determines a good translation and a mediocre one, an equivalent translation and one that is not.

Third: Perfect translation is a *talent*. Because translation is not a uniquely technical activity, it is a conceptual activity, of creation (understandably in the domain of language). Every creation presupposes a talent. Translation as well. We must support Nida who has maintained that quality translation is in fact an art (1974). Perfect translation is not just an apprenticeship of truths and scientific innovations, of literary and artistic values; it is in itself heuristic; it stimulates heuristic thought, the creative and heuristic abilities of the human personality. Thus translation is not just an activity of reproduction but is one of creation which sets free all of the individual's spiritual forces: intellect, intuition, emotions, imagination, will and memory. Like all creative activity, translation makes for the coexistence of the known and the unknown, the common and the unique, the conscious and the unconscious, knowledge and imagination, experience and research.

The translator's talent is measured in view of the reader and so are the results. If a translation is accepted by readers, if it withstands the test of time, if while taking into account the original it maximally enriches the sentiments, experience and ideas of the reader by way of equivalence, adding to them the values and innovations contained in the original, then it can be justifiably stated that the translation is good and is the product of talent.

Fourth: A perfect translation is one which possesses the *best linguistic and stylistic qualities*. The language of the translation depends upon the language of the original. But perfect language in the original does not necessarily mean or guarantee perfect language in the translation. Linguistic and stylistic perfection is the first responsibility of the translator; it cannot be replaced or compensated for by another approach. Language is the blood of translation, that which nourishes all of its cells. Perfect translations are enriching; that is a fact. But they also accelerate the process of every nation's self-development of literary expression.

It is obligatory that different trends in translation theory propose models of perfect translation, emphasizing the demands which stem from their very nature.

Two fundamental approaches can be mentioned in this sense,
—one, with a purely linguistic basis
—the other, purely pragmatic.

The linguistic approach presupposes a correlation between the two linguistic systems, a study from the linguistic level of translation, isolated from other levels. When considering translation as a purely linguistic operation, the meaning and functions of the translated text do not elicit suitable attention.

The pragmatic criterion is based only upon the situation of true communication. It presupposes adequate reactions by the reader. Unfortunately, this criterion does not respond to exceptions and cannot be applied to situations of immaterial character; moreover, it becomes even more complicated afterwards with the possibility of the extralinguistic information being conceived by the reader.

These criteria cannot be applied uniformly to all translation activity. They are formulated and applied as needed at the time of literary or scientific translation, or translation of documents and scholarly works.

The answers to questions about how to use objective criteria in translation are also contradictory.

The appreciation of literary translation can be cited as an extreme case, where frequently the criteria of translation are replaced by aesthetic, psychological, and more often subjective considerations.

Another extreme case would be considerations of quantity, frequently emphasized when it is a matter of pedagogical application, or for translation institutions—in order to calculate the fees of translators.

The evaluation of every complex human activity involves the application of a unique scale of appreciation of vastly different factors. It is the same with the case before us. Our objective is to draw a common denominator from literary, aesthetic, linguistic, pragmatic, and other criteria, resulting in the overall evaluation of translation.

Avoiding subjectivity by using rigorous and obligatory norms would be an experience doomed to failure because:
— such norms cannot entirely reflect all the errors, all the cases which are particular to a given translation,
— such norms would have such an inclusive nature, they would be so abstract that their application would always be influenced by the subjective acceptance of the person in charge of its evaluation.

Subjectivism could not be abandoned by replacing subjective criteria with objective criteria, but by seeking objectivism in the criteria forming the ideal or the concept of perfect translation. In this sense the methods which are applied largely in literary criticism, sociology, and psychological and sociolinguistic research can provide some help.

When we admit that translation is a complex phenomenon showing different aspects—linguistic, substantive, informative, literary, aesthetic, historical, cultural and communicative, we are obliged to admit also that the study of translation presupposes different approaches: linguistic, literary, critical, psychological, etc. What Plato stated is true, one cannot recognize equitation and ignore the horse. Consequently one approach or another cannot be either underestimated, or overestimated, in order to avoid blocking the path of knowledge of the true elements of translation activity and of its multiple structures. Translation necessitates diversified research.

In this sense, *the perfect translation* is that which reflects all the *qualitative characteristics* comprising the phenomenon of translation.

Finally, I would like to emphasize that perfect translation does not just ensue from the demands of the period and the original. The perfect translation depends largely upon the perfect translator. By leaning towards one problem, we reach another: What is the perfect translator? If it were possible to paint a graphic portrait, the dominant traits would be the following:

— love for the profession and faith in the mission of the translator;

— professionalism, linguistic, cultural education, etc., responsibility with respect to work, responsibility vis-à-vis the original and the author;

— diligence, because translation is rewarding but time-consuming work;

— creative ability, ability to provide access to an original work and reconstruct a new linguistic existence of the text;

—love vis-à-vis one's own national literature and that which one is translating;

—intelligence.

The translator must have an aptitude, but also a sense of responsibility; be self-confident, but believe in his mission; be recognized by the general public, but possess all the necessary qualities in order to be so recognized.

At present, at the end of the 20th century, it has become more evident than ever that the exchange of cultural values is a necessary obligation for the evolution of world culture and of national cultures. Translation is a link between eras, between different civilizations and different peoples. This mission can only be accomplished through perfect translation which necessitates two compulsory conditions: on the one hand a talented text, and on the other hand, a talented translator.

I would like to communicate my best wishes for the success of this collection which, through inspiration and direction, is destined to facilitate exchanges as we research the ideal of perfect translation, and of translation activity in general.

REFERENCES

Nida, E. A. "The Nature of Dynamic Equivalence in Translating," FIT Congress *Proceedings* (Montreal, 1977).
——— and Charles R. Taber. *Theory and Practice of Translation.* Leiden; the Netherlands: E. J. Brill, 1974.

Translated by Michele J. Stern

Fidelity in the Hieronymian Sense

GYŐRGY RADÓ

Before 1976 I had translated poetry and prose, fiction and non-fiction; I had written articles on the history and theory of translation; I had edited anthologies. But I had not edited a review. So I had to shape my editorial principles along the way. Two of them are as follows. First, an editor must not abuse his function filling the review with the products of his own brain, but sometimes he must publish his papers too – proving that he is not an outsider. Second, an editor must be liberal: he must not block the way of ideas which do not correspond to his own.

So, I have published several articles by authors who tried to guide the translator towards fidelity by establishing rules on how to translate, especially metaphors, although my own principles about what fidelity is and how the translator should try to attain it were different. My principles, based not on linguistic theories but on my own practice of a half century of translating, have been published under the pretentious title "Outline of Systematic Translatology" (*Babel* 25: 1979, 187–196) where I proposed four guidelines for attaining fidelity in translation: 1) avoid misinterpretation of the source text; 2) since each element of a language is almost never reproducible in another, select in order of their importance those elements of the source text which must be reproduced; 3) compensate for those important elements of the source text which because of the incongruence of the two languages, are not reproducible; 4) find the elegant (or impressive, nice, perhaps artistic) means of expression.

These are, in my opinion, the guidelines for attaining fidelity. But at what kind of fidelity should the translator aim?

Cicero wrote *non verbum pro verbo*, but let us rather refer to St. Jerome who specified the basic principle of translation as follows: *non verbum e verbo, sed sensum exprimere de sensu*, refusing thus literal translation, literal "fidelity," which sometimes still haunts us today. Ten or so years ago, the bulletin of our Canadian colleagues published a caricature of this principle: a customer rejected an English translation because it contained one word less than the French original.

For an example of non-literal translation which I prefer to call Hieronymian, I present a stanza by Paul Verlaine and Árpád Tóth's version, considered in Hungary as the perfect model of poetic translation, along with a literal English translation of Tóth's translation:

Les sanglots longs	Ősz húrja zsong,	Autumn's string hums
Des violons	Jajong, busong	Moans, mourns
De l'automne	A tájon	In the land
Blessent mon coeur	S ont monoton	And pours a monotone
D'une langueur	Bút konokon	Sorrow obstinate
Monotone.	És fájón.	And pained.

Very few words of the source text have their equivalents in the target text (autumn, monotone), there are very few similarities (*violons* – string; *sanglots* – moans; *langueur* – sorrow; *blessent* – pained), but the message of the two texts, their atmosphere and music (including their rhyme, rhythm, and even the phonetic effect of single words) exemplify a translation of *Hieronymian fidelity*.

The four criteria mentioned above (comprehension, selection, compensation, expression) are guidelines, not rules. Rules for translation do not exist, solutions are individual, and must be found in any case by the individual translator.

ATA Accreditation and Excellence in Practice

BEN TEAGUE

The American Translators Association has developed a method of defining and measuring excellence in translation. In the context of this annual, both ATA members and other language professionals may benefit from a treatment of the principles and techniques adopted in the accreditation program. I will therefore begin this essay with a quick history of the effort and a short outline of the methods of testing and evaluation.

Inception of the Program

Several ATA members went to work around 1970 to devise a way of certifying the professional qualifications of translators (the term "accreditation" may have been an unfortunate choice of that group). The committee, under the leadership of Dr. Eliot Beach, had its first exams ready (in French, German, and Spanish into English and English into Spanish) by 1973, and in that and the following year members of the Association took tests at ATA national meetings. In 1974 Russian to English was added; since then the program has grown to take in Portuguese, Polish, and Italian to English and English to all seven partner languages.

Those first exams resembled, in several respects, the ones being given today. Each test consisted of five passages in the appropriate source language, each passage running between 200 and 250 words. In each set of five, one text came from a literary work; one, from a scientific, medical or engineering publication; three, from a variety of nonspecialist sources. The committee selected materials originally published in the source language and did not edit except to provide equivalents for a few obscure items of terminology.

Candidates for accreditation arrived at the exam room with pens and dictionaries. (From the beginning, the ATA placed no restrictions on such resources.) At the start of the test period, each candidate was given a set of five passages and a supply of writing paper. Each person was to choose and translate any three of the five texts in three hours. A proctor kept time and maintained order in the room.

The candidates identified their papers with code numbers supplied by the committee. Each translated passage was photocopied twice and each copy sent to a committee member for grading. Only the committee head could sort out candidates and codes; what is more, the graders were not identified to the candidates or to each other. The graders worked under standards established by the committee; I will take up these later. The committee head received the marked papers and reported the outcomes to the candidates. From the first, the committee made it a rule not to allow appeals or enter into discussion about test results; marked papers have *not* been returned to candidates.

Development

The years since 1974 have seen a few changes in the accreditation program. First, it is much bigger than it was; the committee requires over 100 people to select and grade tests in its 14 language combinations (Japanese-English and other pairs may be added soon). Second, exam passages have grown longer, to an average of 250–280 words (source-language count). Third, the committee now selects five passages under five headings (legal, literary, scientific, technical, "general") instead of three. Fourth, all graders (except in newly introduced language pairs) are themselves accredited.

Perhaps the most vital changes, however, are two having to do with the place the program holds in the world and in the ATA. After knowing but not admitting it for a long time, the committee recently made public its belief that the testing program, even with its 50–60% failure rate, can identify proficient translators only at a "minimal" level. That is, aspirants who are just ready to enter the profession routinely pass exams, while those who fail have not demonstrated even "entry-level" skills.[1] And a 1983 by-laws revision made accreditation part of the

Association's structure for good and all (as a prerequisite for voting membership).

In a sense, then, the accreditation program has come to a self-aware maturity. Through all the changes of the past 12 years, however, the basic techniques of testing and evaluation have remained relatively unchanged, as has the logic guiding the committee in its operations. Since both the techniques and the logic bear on the ATA's working definition of excellence, let me take those up next.

Procedures and Standards

The grading procedure is quickly described: For each passage, the grader reads the work against the original text, marks major and minor errors as defined in the standards, totals up the errors, and applies a scale to get a final mark. The committee head receives the same passage as marked by two graders. If both say "pass," the work gets a pass; if both say "fail," a failing mark. If the two graders differ, the passage goes to a third committee member. Of the three passages attempted, the candidate must pass two in order to become accredited.

The objectivity of the program—and the committee does claim objectivity in its work—rests, then, on the way in which errors are defined. "Major" errors include gross mistranslation, in which the meaning of the original is lost altogether; omission of vital words or other information; insertion of information not contained in the original; inclusion of alternate translations, where the translator should have made a choice; and any important failure in target-language grammar. A candidate who commits two major errors in one passage earns a failing mark for that text.

"Minor" errors include mistranslation that distorts somewhat, but does not wholly falsify, the intent of the original; omission of "words that contribute only slightly to meaning"; presentation of alternate translations where the terms offered are synonyms or nearly so; and "inelegancy" in target-language grammar. A translation may contain an unlimited number of minor errors and still receive a passing grade. A combination of one major and seven minor errors, however, results in a failing mark, and few candidates commit flocks of minor errors without slipping in at least one major one.

The first striking implication in these definitions is that a rather poor translation—grammatically lame, done by a translator unsure of terminology and careless in checking, perhaps even with a key term badly rendered—can still earn a "pass." It is true, also, that a fairly good translation, even one by an accomplished professional, but marred by an omitted clause and a misread word, can properly be marked "fail." To critics who say that the program is failing to identify "good" and "bad" translators, the committee responds that it can evaluate only the translation that was produced during the test, not the training—or the prospects—of the candidate.

Negative Formulation

But a second implication perhaps tells more about the logic (I would not say "philosophy") of the accreditation program. The committee's standards are doubly negative. The committee has defined a "minimally proficient" translator as one who can *avoid* making certain types and numbers of mistakes; the standards in effect represent a denial of, or at least resistance to, any identification of "skills" in the translating profession.

The history of the program suggests that such resistance, if it was not conscious, was still real. Dr. Beach and many of the members of his first committee called themselves "working translators" as distinct from linguists and teachers. Two common patterns in the backgrounds of working translators in the U.S. are, or were until recently, (1) little formal training, varied experience, little present contact with the academic world; (2) formal training in an institution abroad, steady employment in translating, little present contact with the academic world. In 1973 few working translators would have looked to teachers of languages or linguistics for help in evaluating the efforts of other translators. What is more, the aim of the first Accreditation Committee was to provide a means of recognition for translators among themselves; assessment by those outside the Association may not have been regarded as desirable or even acceptable.

It may be natural, too, for a translator who has gained much professional knowledge, bit by painful bit, to resist the idea of translating as the systematic practice of now this skill, now that. Too much analysis, such a translator might fear, could turn a smooth and rhythmical operation, though one not well understood, into an awkward and joyless exercise.

Whatever its members' motivations, the ATA finally produced an evaluation program that not only declines to test comprehension, composition, and translation skills separately, but actually declares vocabulary knowledge to be an adjunct to the true, central and unitary skill of. . .translating.

Positive Implications

It would be wrong to leave the impression that the ATA or the Accreditation Committee regards the accreditation program as a negative one. The expressed aim of the program has always been to conduct performance testing of translators, that is, to simulate the conditions under which professional translators work and the demands that they must meet. From the first, the exam situation has been as relaxed as the committee and the proctors could make it; candidates may bring with them the books and materials they customarily use, may leave the room during the exam, and may revise and discard their work as they wish. On the other hand, a test room can never reproduce a real translator's working conditions; other people are present, it is not usually possible to type, and even the stoutest translator can bring to the exam only a fraction of his or her professional library. What is more, *taking a test* is an unnatural situation for the translator, and some candidates react badly to perceived and real pressures. These considerations, incidentally, provide the correct light in which to view the "lenient" grading standards: No one in the ATA would maintain that it is all right to commit a major error, or even a minor one, when working under accustomed conditions, but under the artificial constraints of the testing period some lapses may be excused.

Finally, the accreditation program has sought to make a virtue of what may once have been a necessity. If we cannot discern what "skills" we are practicing, and if we might not wish to in any case, we ask candidates to do something that bears on their professional life, something we can evaluate: translate a text. The aims of the program are narrow, but the Association considers them worthwhile and attainable.

In its first ten years, the accreditation program found wide acceptance among ATA members. Accreditation was made an alternative route to full membership by 1978; in 1983, as I stated earlier, it became a principal qualification. The number of exams given is approaching the total number of members, though many have taken multiple exams and some have taken none. The committee has experienced pressure to expand the selection of languages offered.

Perhaps a more telling sign is the seemingly wide acceptance of a plan for advanced professional certification, first advanced by Henry Fischbach and now under intensive development.[2] Although the new program will seek to identify highly (not "minimally") proficient translators as to both language pair and subject specialty, the ATA's good experience with accreditation has led to the adoption of a similar testing arrangement: translation of material from the recent source-language literature and grading against a performance standard. The accreditation program has been of value to the Association and will continue to be central to ATA life, both in itself and in its "offspring."

NOTES

1. That is, although these candidates may possess the skills, they have not demonstrated them. See the discussion of testing conditions and their effect on performance ("Positive Implications").

2. The advanced certification program will not supplant the existing program but supplement it. Accreditation will remain the requirement for voting membership; certification will probably appeal to a relatively small number of veteran translators.

Professionalism in Academic Programs

RICHARD BROD

Academic practitioners of the humanities have traditionally been unwilling to codify, let alone quantify, learning outcomes and
professional standards of performance and achievement in their fields.
To the extent that foreign language faculty are part of the humanities,
this generalization certainly applies to them, but it is also true that
their field does not conform precisely to the classic norms of the
humanities, at least to the extent that their departments teach not
merely a body of knowledge, but also a usable skill. In theory they,
unlike other humanists, ought to be able to quantify both their learning outcomes and their professional standards. Yet there are other
obstacles which might prevent this from happening.

Apart from the natural fragmentation of their field, language faculty have difficulty reaching consensus on a definition of their function
in American schools and colleges. For some, language study belongs
to the humanities and to general education: its role is to give students
an experience of a foreign language and culture, both specifically and
generically. For others, the role of language study in modern education is to give students the practical communicative skills they need
to live in an interdependent world. Clearly, the two roles can coexist:
both have noble objectives, and both rest upon a refreshingly ideal-
ized view of human learning and human potential. Yet the differences
are not easily reconciled.

In recent years foreign language faculty have had to make a major
shift in their thinking. When their only function in education was traditional and humanistic, they could conduct their courses and programs
as they chose, serving their students by serving their texts. With the
new emphasis on practical, communicative skills, they now had to pay

attention to students' real-life needs. In many ways the adjustment has been painful. Preoccupied with the still fragile (and eroding) language requirement and the classic two-year sequence intended to fulfill it, how much thought have language faculty traditionally given to the real needs of language users? Have they ever questioned the relationship between investment of effort and payoff? Have they ever tried to calculate precisely how many hours of drill, practice, exposure, and reinforcement it might take before a student could ask for the proverbial cup of coffee in French, deal with a potential customer in Spanish, listen to a lecture in German? Have they tried to hold themselves to a standard of efficiency or accountability? Some teachers in other fields can do this relatively easily; surely foreign language faculty can make an effort to do it as well.

Ultimately, they have little choice. While they may disapprove of those who believe it possible to run an educational institution like a business, such views are pervasive and influential. And language faculty themselves have much to gain from seeking a rational basis for measuring achievement in language study. In this sense the oral proficiency "movement" now in vogue is far more than merely another bandwagon for teachers to follow.[1] If it continues as it should to lead its adherents in the right direction, it can become nothing less than a joyous revolution in foreign language study in the United States.

Along with a revolutionary new way of measuring and defining expectations has come a shift in content. Often to the regret of those who cherish literature above all other values, a growing number of academic language departments have developed preprofessional courses—and in some cases degree programs—to meet the real-life, practical needs of language learners. Some courses have focused on science and technology; some have linked with other academic specialties or with the arts; others, especially in Spanish, have served the needs of working-class students pursuing occupational training; a few have undertaken to prepare professional translators; and a remarkable number have concentrated on business. All have had a practical focus; all have recognized the necessity to serve an external standard of performance and accountability.

On the whole, the broadening of curricular offerings to include practical and preprofessional training as well as traditional courses is a good thing, but it places a special burden on language faculty. Clearly it is now to their advantage to (1) clarify and reconcile the dichotomy between the two objectives before the gap between them becomes un-bridgeable, and (2) articulate standards of quality and performance ex-pectations in as much detail as possible. While the bulk of this work must occur in the classroom, the so-called leadership echelons in the field must take a major share of the responsibility. The Modern Language Association and other organizations should continue to ex-plore ways in which they can advise and guide their constituents in the arts of self-examination and self-evaluation and begin to exercise some moral or persuasive power over the many disparate programs in the field.[2] Commitment to the principle of academic freedom for both individuals and departments need not lead to anarchy; healthy diversity should not lead to chaos.

Traditionally, service organizations like MLA, ACTFL, and AATSP avoid making judgments of academic programs in the field; traditionally, they leave to others (e.g., the College Board, Educational Testing Ser-vice, and commercial publishers of guidebooks) the task of describing or evaluating programs. While this division of labor is likely to per-sist, the needs of consumers, and of the profession itself, would prob-ably be better served if leadership organizations were to take greater responsibility for monitoring and advising than is now the case. Until that happens, the profession will have to live with a situation in which its own standards are less well defined than those of many representa-tives of other professions who become consumers of its products. Like the proverbial bridesmaids who seek to become brides, language pro-fessionals need to find ways to be more assertive and decisive about their own destinies.

NOTES

1. The oral proficiency "movement," spearheaded by the American Council on the Teaching of Foreign Languages, has been concerned with adapting definitions and standards developed by the Foreign Service Institute and other government schools for use in civilian schools and colleges, and with training foreign language faculty to administer and evaluate oral interview tests.

2. Along these lines the MLA's Association of Departments of English published in 1985 a pamphlet entitled *A Checklist and Guide for Reviewing Departments of English*; and the Association of Departments of Foreign Languages published "A Checklist for Self-Study for Departments of Languages and Literatures" (*ADFL Bulletin* 16.3 (1985), 45–53. Ed. Note: The address of the MLA is 10 Astor Place, New York, NY 10003.

The Proposed ATA Program Accreditation

PETER W. KRAWUTSCHKE

It is not the purpose of this paper to plead the case of pro-grammatic accreditation by the American Translators Association (ATA) for the ever-increasing number of programs actually or allegedly preparing foreign language students for professional work in transla-tion. This has been done elsewhere.[1] Nor shall this paper deal with the subject matter of "accreditation" which is so unique and occasionally troublesome to the educational system in the United States. That, too, has been done prolifically elsewhere.[2]

What shall be discussed is the process and the criteria by which the major US professional organization representing the field of transla-tion could bring its members' considerable knowledge and expertise to bear on the design, operation, and performance of educational pro-grams in translation. By doing so, the ATA could assume the role of an important link between the professional world of applied foreign languages and Academia. All of this presupposes, of course, that there is a professional world for the field of translation rather than merely an industry and that there is something of substance in Academia to be evaluated, approved, or "accredited."

Basic to the evaluation of translator training programs by a profes-sional organization is the assumption that translation is a profession, that it is based on a body of knowledge and skills transmittable and augmentable at a setting usually afforded to other professions at a university, and that this academic process is open to quantitative and qualitative evaluation and judgments, particularly in the fields of technical and scientific translation.

Of course, there are substantial forces opposed to the implementation of any type of evaluation or standard-setting approach to translator training.

On the one hand, academic institutions usually, but not always, object to interference in internal matters by outside organizations. And there is, to be sure, a very delicate balance between academic freedom and the demands by society for adequate performance, especially in those areas in which academic performance can have an observable and measurable impact. This resistance may be particularly true for those disciplines which usually sponsor translator training programs; e.g., foreign language departments, merged foreign language and Linguistics departments, and Comparative Literature departments. These academic units generally have no experience with programmatic accreditation by professional organizations, and occasionally may be only vaguely aware that they are capable of creating academic illusions.

On the other hand, opposition to the ATA's involvement in program accreditation may also come from individual practicing translators and from some segments of the translation industry. After all, one may be able to assume that most translators presently plying their trade do so without benefit of substantial postsecondary education in the field of translation. Frequently the effects of the vicissitudes of life are mistaken for talent and as a demonstration for the non-sequitur of university training. For many ATA members these and other factors result in a considerable lack of understanding and appreciation of the interplay between professions and university in this country. In addition, any industry tends to regard with suspicion those social trends which might eventually lead to an increase in the cost of the human element involved in the production process.

With these provisos in mind and assuming a fortuitous confluence of enlightenment and good will by all factions involved, it ought to be possible to construct a system of "accreditation," or "approval,"[3] or even "registration"[4] for educational programs in translator training within a reasonable period of time. Such a process is described in the following pages.

The opinions and procedures suggested below are those of the author and not those of the ATA. It is hoped that the following proposal[5] will serve as a point of departure for opposing views to generate a substantive discussion, and that it will eventually yield an applicable synthesis, while at the same time elucidating those areas of our profession which need further study, research, and description.

The Accrediting Body

Central to initiating a system of accreditation by a professional organization is the creation of an organizational entity, a body, to assume responsibility and to give direction to the process. This ATA Committee on Accreditation of Educational Programs in Translator Training should be a standing, autonomous committee of the ATA. It should consist of at least five members appointed by the ATA Board of Directors to staggered terms of three years. Reappointment should not be precluded. The chair of the committee should also be appointed by the ATA Board.

To assure a balanced evaluation of programs, the committee of five members should be composed of three members representing schools with existing translator training programs (peer evaluation) and two members from private or governmental practice. Should programs in literary translation be included in this process, one of the three members representing existing translator training programs should be appointed by the American Literary Translators Association (ALTA). A larger committee should be similarly composed.

Responsibility of the Accrediting Body

The Committee on Accreditation of Educational Programs in Translator Training would be charged with the responsibility of formulating, reviewing, implementing, and operating the accreditation program of the Association. Its initial task would be to secure sufficient funding to support a considerable research and administrative undertaking. The committee's policies, guidelines, and standards and criteria as well as final action on accreditation would be subject to review and approval by the ATA Board of Directors.

Procedures Used in Accreditation

The following individual steps and criteria would be involved in the accreditation of an individual program. A program seeking accreditation should have been in operation at least two years prior to requesting ATA accreditation. At the same time, it should be part of those areas of an institution of higher learning accredited by a regional accrediting organization. The process of evaluation should be initiated only after the highest administrative officer of the institution sponsoring the program has made a formal request to the Committee on Accreditation for an on-site visit. After payment of an administrative fee (the committee would have to set an amount commensurate with the actual administrative cost and comparable to the charges made by similar professional accrediting bodies) and receipt of the formal request, the Committee on Accreditation would then request the completion of a programmatic self-study report by the university official in charge of the translator training program. Upon its return to the Committee on Accreditation, this report would then be evaluated by the members of the committee. If the majority of the committee approves an on-site visitation, the chair of the committee will appoint a visiting team from the committee's membership and will appoint the team's chair. It is suggested that the team consist of two educators and one practicing translator; minimally and to be cost effective, it should consist of one educator and one practitioner. The sponsoring school would assume the cost for travel and maintenance of the members of the visiting team.

During the visit, which would last two or three days, the visiting team would apply the Association's accreditation standards to the program to be evaluated in terms of published program objectives, curriculum, faculty, students, administration, financial support, physical facilities including an evaluation of library holdings and accessibility. These individual areas of evaluation shall be discussed later in more detail.

Following the visit, the chair of the visiting team writes his report. After approval by the other members of the team, the factual portion of the report is transmitted to the initiating official of the institution visited for his verification and response. These two documents would then form the basis for the team's final report. Prior to taking action on the visiting team's report and recommendation, the Committee on Accreditation should send the school a copy of the final report and give it an opportunity to respond to it. A majority vote of the committee should be required in order to recommend to the ATA Board of Directors that the program evaluated be granted "accreditation."

The final decision on accreditation would rest with the ATA Board of Directors which could act on the recommendations made by the

Committee on Accreditation during its meeting at the Annual ATA Conference. Should accreditation be denied, an institution could file a written appeal with the ATA Board of Directors which then should appoint a special committee to consider the appeal.

Accredited programs should be subject to review by a visiting team every five years. Major programmatic changes should trigger earlier reviews.

A list of ATA accredited programs could be published annually in the *ATA Chronicle* and could be made available to the public, in particular to high school[6] and college advisors. Information as to whether a program not on the list of accredited programs had been under consideration for ATA accreditation would not be made available.

Standards and Criteria of Evaluation

The standards and criteria involved in the evaluation of individual programs would have to be developed. It is assumed that they would not depart considerably from the five general areas of evaluation usually included in the process of accreditation, i.e., curriculum, faculty, students, program administration, and institutional commitment. The criteria by which standards would be applied must be able to distinguish between translator training programs at the graduate and undergraduate level. In both cases the assumption should be that language skills are prerequisites to the program and not part of the program. It is the hope of this author that the goals of translator training would not be confused with those of foreign language pedagogy; in other words, translator training programs should not have language learning as one of their primary functions. Criteria would also have to distinguish between programs in general, technical and scientific, or literary translation since each one of these program types involves different expectations in terms of student and faculty performance and institutional support.

The Curricular Content of a Program

There is growing consensus that university trained translators should have a good understanding of the ethics, the history and the theory of translation, of the legal and business aspects of the profession, and of the impact of new technologies on the field. This, of course, in addition to work in translation, terminology, lexicography, and linguistics. Surely, these items would be included in a standard for curricular content. At the graduate level, some of these topics should be allotted their own course; e.g., one could insist that a course in terminology and one in theory be included in the program. In addition, it seems unavoidable, at least in a non-literary translation program, that a course in computer assisted translation be included eventually. And all programs would have to be evaluated in terms of their entry requirements not only in the source language or languages but also in English. Here, too, there seems to be a growing consensus that it should not be the function of translator training programs to teach English.

If one accepts the tenet that translation is essentially a unidirectional, language-pair specific process, the committee would have to take a close look at the cost-effective method of having one multi-language, field-specific course taught by one instructor. At the same time the committee would have to ascertain at what level translation into a foreign language becomes realistic in terms of professionally acceptable performance standards. One may marvel, for example, at the courage of the foreign language teaching profession when it offers business German, French, or Spanish courses to undergraduates who still have difficulties writing acceptable English.

In addition, the committee might wish to include in its standards the requirement of a substantial practicum or internship. In spite of the fact that these practica or internships are most difficult to organize, initiate, and sustain,[7] there is growing national and international agreement among professionals in translator training that such internships should be an integral part of any translator training program.[8] The committee might be well guided to follow the findings of Kaston's *Preparing Humanists for Work: A National Study of Undergraduate Internships in the Humanities* in establishing its criteria for acceptable internship or practicum experiences.[9] Questions which would have to be addressed are: How is the internship integrated into the program? Is it a period of experience in professional practice over an extended period of time under careful professional supervision or is it merely an incidental work experience employing some foreign language skills? In other words, how is the student's work evaluated and does the evaluation enhance the learning process?

Furthermore, the committee would have to arrive at some guidelines in reference to the sequential development of the curriculum, the appropriate length of particular translator training programs, as well as the credentialing of the training received.

For example, there are few who would argue that it is essential that a student have a good knowledge of the source language and culture, and of the sciences, and of technical writing in English before beginning the process of learning technical translation. However, should he have a course *about* translation before or after this practical work? And should a final examination conclude the whole program?

The appropriate length of study also needs to be established. Could an undergraduate program in translator training consist of a minor of twenty semester hours (without including pure foreign language courses) or should no fewer than thirty semester hours (usually a major) be required? Or are both options possible? The MA degree, of course, would generally consist of at least thirty semester hours of course work. Fortunately some valuable information to assist in dealing with these questions will be forthcoming from research presently being conducted by the Translation Research and Instruction Program at SUNY Binghamton.

And finally, the committee would have to examine the administrative impact of the thesis that degrees in translator training, particularly with technical and scientific specialization, ought to be separable and separate from foreign language degrees. This author is not impressed by courses and programs which have not gone through the laborious curricular approval process which all other college or university courses must traverse before they find their place in the official offerings announced in a catalog or bulletin. Hence, he does not consider undergraduate certificates presented by departmental chairs or deans appropriate degrees for serious professional or preprofessional educational experience. The goal for the profession should be to foster MA's in Translation, BA's with majors and minors in translation. And all of them clearly labeled as such on a student's academic transcript.

While setting all these minimum standards and criteria, the Committee on Accreditation will consistently need to strive to allow for sound individual variations and for curricular experimentation and innovation.

Faculty

The second area for which the Committee on Accreditation would write standards is that of the faculty involved in translator training programs. A look at many programs in operation at the present time indicates that a considerable number of younger, probably untenured, faculty are involved. In most cases this is professional suicide for the individuals concerned unless policy statements on promotion and tenure or individual appointments clearly stipulate that "translation" is a desired professional activity. In most cases research and publication in the traditional foreign language areas will continue to be required by faculty committees for tenure and promotion to assistant or associate professor; certainly for promotion to full professor. Hence programs depending exclusively on the labors of young, untenured, or not promotable associate professors should be carefully evaluated.

The criteria in this area should insist that full-time faculty hold degrees comparable to their peers', i.e., PhD's. Faculty should possess practical experience in the field, demonstrated through publications, published and unpublished translations—of a technical or scientific nature if involved in a technical or scientific translator training program. It should not be acceptable that a teacher of first- or second-year foreign language courses automatically qualifies as a teacher of technical or scientific translation. And, of course, an acceptable student-faculty ratio should be stated—1:15, for example, might not be an overly ambitious goal to strive for in an area as complicated as translation. Some consideration would have to be given to the composite individual work-load of faculty involved in the translation program, i.e., the ratio between teaching, research, administrative tasks, and participation in professional work (translations!), and professional societies.

One of the key items that would have to be evaluated under this rubric is staffing with part-time faculty. Any program that is essentially staffed by part-time help—many times not appointed by the governing board of the institution—should be evaluated with great care. While it is frequently necessary for universities to employ non-academic specialists in emerging fields in which the institution is not yet com-

petently staffed, a permanent solution through part-time faculty is usually a financial arrangement beneficial to the institution[10] and reserved
for the academic fringes. The Committee on Accreditation should
definitely look at new appointments in the department sponsoring the
translation program and at continuing use of part-time staff.

The Student Body

Under this rubric, primary areas of concern for the Committee on
Accreditation would be admission standards such as prerequisite
minimal foreign language and English skills which should be
demonstrated at the beginning of the program. Acceptable ways to
evaluate these skills need to be discussed; however, an initial essay,
ACT, SAT, GRE scores, or courses transferred from other institutions with sufficiently good grades should give an indication of required
remedial work or non-acceptance into the program.

Beyond the academic preparation for a particular program, the committee should look at the retention of students and how effective and
straightforward academic advising is in relation to published information available to students. Of course, the committee would definitely
want to examine the record of the graduates of the program in order
to ascertain if they have found employment in the field or related areas,
or if they have gone on to further academic study or professional practice. This type of information would be a good indicator of the program's effectiveness and success in reaching its stated goals.

Program Administration

The Committee on Accreditation would probably want to specify
that the program be an addressable entity within the institution, with
a specified individual in charge of the program, and a set of policies
and programmatic goals. It may even wish to insist that there be an
advisory board or committee with a mix of educators and practicing
translators. In addition, there should be a clear administrative and
curricular chain of communication and responsibility for the program.
The committee's criteria may also include that a history of the program be available.

Institutional Commitment

The Committee on Accreditation should design the means to elicit and record a clear indication that the institution is financially and philosophically supportive of its translator training program. Particularly in the present times of financial hardships for higher education, this should not involve unreasonable expenditures; however, no academic program can function meaningfully without basic support.

One indicator of non-monetary institutional support consists of intra- and interdepartmental faculty involvement in the program or of publicity about the program in various press releases and interinstitutional means of communication.

Basic financial support other than faculty salaries includes allocations for travel money, publishing support for translations and translation-related research, public events and announcements involving the translation program.

Another equally important documentation of institutional commitment the committee may wish to consider is the inclusion of "translation" in personnel policy statements dealing with appointment, tenure, and promotion.

Perhaps the most simple area to evaluate yet the most difficult to describe in normative terms is that of physical resources available to the program. Yet this area is an important indicator of institutional commitment. The difficulty in implementing a standard in this area will be based on the need to reach a consensus on itemized lists of basic required items. While most of us agree that appropriate office and classroom space be available, further discussion will be needed in reference to the basic equipment that should be available to students and faculty in a translation program. This antiquated translator still works initially with pencil and yellow notepaper. He would fit amiably into any equipment and supply budget. But his students would not fit into any productive translation setting. Do we require typing, WP, CAT skills? If yes, will the equipment be furnished by the school? Do we wish to require dictating machine experience? Should a photocopying machine be available? The Committee on Accreditation would have to take a position on these seemingly trivial matters.

Equally important would be the committee's deliberations on the maintenance of library resources for the program to be evaluated. All professional organizations evaluating programs in their respective fields give more than a cursory glance at the library or libraries that support the program. For a program that offers general work in translation a supporting library might contain the following volumes of secondary literature[11]: Brislin's *Translation. Applications and Research,* Brower's *On Translation,* Catford's *A Linguistic Theory of Translation,* Congrat-Butlar's *Translation and Translators. An International Directory and Guide,* House's *A Model for Translation Quality Assessment,* Kelly's *The True Interpreter,* Mounin's *Les problèmes théoriques de la traduction,* Newmark's *Approaches to Translation,* Vázquez-Ayora's *Introducción a la traductología,* and Willss' *Übersetzungswissenschaft.*

Of course, the informed reader will immediately have noticed several omissions in the above sample inventory. At least Nida's *Toward a Science of Translation,* Steiner's *After Babel,* Savory's *The Art of Translation,* Levy's *Die literarische Übersetzung,* Larson's *Meaning-based Translation,* and Rose's ever so useful *Translation Spectrum* should have been included in addition to the proceedings of the recently instituted ATA Conferences.

One would also want to make certain that at least the *ATA Chronicle, Babel, The Incorporated Linguist, Lebende Sprachen, Meta,* and *Traduire* be available to students in the program. Similarly, a basic collection of articles on "translation" ought to be at hand if the journals themselves are not available.

The same applies to basic dictionary, glossary, and encyclopedia collections. For example, a program that purports to teach German to English technical and scientific translation should at least have "Ernst," "Walther," and "DeVries" available in addition to, perhaps, McGraw-Hill's *Dictionary of Scientific and Technical Terms* as well as some DIN, ASTM, and SAE norms, standards, and procedures.

These minimal general and field and language-pair specific inventories need to be constructed by surveys of our practicing ATA members and should be periodically up-dated.[12] They would be essential for the work of the Committee on Accreditation as well as of interest to the public at large.

Furthermore, the committee might wish to ascertain that there exists sufficient funding for interlibrary loan requests, for usage of various data bases, and for new acquisitions. And it would want to establish student usage of these library resources.

These, and other areas of concern would or could be included in an accreditation (or approval or registration) process of educational programs in translator training. While meeting some of these standards and criteria would certainly create hardships for marginal programs, those programs with a longstanding and excellent academic record should welcome such concern on part of a professional organization representing their field. And all ATA members should insist on minimal standards of competency for those who enter their profession and for those who teach them.

Finally, as it goes about its task of writing standards and compiling criteria, the Committee on Accreditation would undoubtedly keep in mind that the ultimate criterion for judging a program in translator training is whether it produces competent graduates who enter the profession and perform effectively.[13]

NOTES

1. See Krawutschke, "Translation as an Academic Discipline: Opportunities and Dangers for the Profession." See Reference below.

2. Initial reading might consist of The Council of Postsecondary Accreditation's *The Balance Wheel for Accreditation* and *Accreditation of Graduate Education: A Joint Policy Statement*, as well as *The Journal of Higher Education* 50 (March/April 1979).

3. Program approval by a professional organization usually means that a program is able to demonstrate that it has fulfilled specified requirements and conditions. It is a less formal and less expensive process which could be conducted without on-site visitation.

4. Program registration simply means that an institution offers a defined program of study as it is described and that a periodically up-dated record of such programs is kept by a national professional organization.

5. This proposal follows an outline prepared in 1979 by the then existing ATA Committee on Accreditation of Educational Programs in Translator Training which was chaired by the author.

6. It should be pointed out that "(430) Interpreting/translating" is now one of the career options available to high school seniors in the *1984–85 Student Bulletin for SAT and Achievement Tests* under the heading "Fields of Study in Two-and Four-year Colleges and Career Choices," p. 10.

7. See Wilss, *Are Training Programs for Translators Keeping up With the Times?*, p. 2.

8. The author appreciates Prof. Gustave Cammaert's (Chair of the FIT Committee for Training and Qualification of Translators) courtesy of furnishing him with the synthesis of his 1983 survey on "The Training of Translators and Interpreters." See also articles by Woodsworth and Brisset.

9. For a summary of this study see *Academic Leader* pp. 1–2.

10. A brief computation may serve as an illustration: At the author's university a new PhD in foreign languages can be "had" for $19,000 (!) for an academic year appointment. Fringe benefits are not included in this amount. The same teaching load can be covered by part-time staff for $9,600 at a savings to the university of $9,400.

11. The following listing is to serve only as an illustration for the purposes of this paper. Consult Bausch or Hoof for exhaustive bibliographic inventories.

12. Fortunately, an excellent and exemplary inventory prepared by Gillmeier and Wright already exists for the field of German-English technical translation illustrated in the above sample.

13. See Standard 6.1 of National Council for Accreditation of Teacher Education pp. 10–11.

REFERENCES

ATA Committee on Accreditation of Education Programs. "Draft of Policies and Criteria for the Accreditation of Education Programs in Translator Training." Unpublished report, 1979, rev. 1983.

Bausch, Karl R., Josef Klegraf, and Wolfram Wilss. *The Science of Translation: An Analytical Bibliography.* 2 vols. Vol. I 1962–1969, Vol. II 1970–1971. Tübingen: Gunter Narr, 1970 and 1972.

Brislin, Richard, ed. *Translation. Applications and Research.* New York: Gardener Press, 1976.

Brisset, Annie. "Integrating Practical Training in the Curriculum – The Canadian Experience." *Proceedings of the 26th Annual Conference of the American Translators Association.* Ed. Patricia E. Newman. Medford, N.J.: Learned Information, Inc., 1985. 277–284.

Brower, Reuben, ed. *On Translation.* Cambridge, MA: Harvard, 1954, rpt. 1966.

Cammaert, Gustave. "Training of Translators and Interpreters. Results of an Enquiry." Letter to author. 2 November 1983.

Catford, John C. *A Linguistic Theory of Translation: An Essay in Applied Linguistics.* London: Oxford University Press, 1965.

College Entrance Examination Board. *1984–85 Student Bulletin for SAT and Achievement Tests.* Princeton, NJ: Educational Testing Service, 1984.

Congrat-Butlar, Stefan. *Translation and Translators: An International Directory and Guide.* New York: Bowker, 1979.

Council on Postsecondary Accreditation. *The Balance Wheel for Accreditation.* Washington: COPA, 1983.

Council on Postsecondary Accreditation and The Council of Graduate Schools in the United States. *Accreditation of Graduate Education: A Joint Policy Statement.* Washington: CGS, 1978.

"Departments and Internships," *Academic Leader* Sept. 1985: 1–2.

DeVries, Louis and Theo M. Herrmann. *German–English/English–German Technical and Engineering Dictionary.* 2 vols. New York: McGraw-Hill, 1972.

Ernst, Richard. *Dictionary of Engineering and Technology: German–English/English–German.* 4th ed. 2 vols. New York: Oxford University Press, 1980.

Gillmeier, Ingrid and Sue Ellen Wright. "The German/English Translator's Toolbox: A Critical Bibliography for Mechanical & Manufacturing Engineering." *Proceedings of the 26th Annual Conference of the American Translators Association.* Ed. Patricia E. Newman. Medford, NJ: Learned Information, Inc., 1985.

Hoof, Henri van. *Internationale Bibliographie der Übersetzung. International Bibliography of Translation.* Pullach bei München: Verlag Dokumentation, 1973.

House, Juliane. A Model for Translation Quality Assessment. Tübingen: Gunter Narr, 1977.

Journal of Higher Education. 50 (1979): 115–232.

Kaston, Carren O. with James M. Heffernan. Preparing Humanists for Work: A National Study of Undergraduate Internships in the Humanities. Washington: The Washington Center, 1984.

Kelly, Louis G. The True Interpreter: A History of Translation Theory and Practice in the West. New York: St. Martin's Press, 1979.

Krawutschke, Peter. "Translation as an Academic Discipline: Opportunities and Dangers for the Profession." Proceedings of the 25th Annual Conference of the American Translators Association. Ed. Patricia E. Newman. Medford, NJ: Learned Information, Inc. 1984.

Larsen, Mildred. Meaning-based Translation: A Guide to Cross-language Equivalence. Lanham, Md.: University Presses of America, 1984.

Levý, Jirí. Die literarische Übersetzung. Theorie einer Kunstgattung. Trans. Walter Schamschula. Frankfurt a.M., Bonn: Athenäum, 1969.

McGraw-Hill Dictionary of Scientific and Technical Terms. New York: McGraw-Hill, 1976.

Mounin, Georges. Les problèmes théoriques de la traduction. Paris: Gallimard, 1963.

National Council for Accreditation of Teacher Education. Standards for the Accreditation of Teacher Education. Washington: NCATE, 1977.

Newman, Patricia E., ed. Proceedings of the 25th Annual Conference of the American Translators Association. Medford, NJ: Learned Information, Inc., 1984.

———. Proceedings of the 26th Annual Conference of the American Translators Association. Medford, NJ: Learned Information, Inc., 1985.

Newmark, Peter. Approaches to Translation. New York: Pergamon Press, 1981.

Nida, Eugene A. Toward a Science of Translating, With Special Reference to Principles and Procedures Involved in Bible Translating. Leiden: Brill, 1964.

Rose, Marilyn Gaddis, ed. Translation Spectrum: Essays on Theory and Practice. Albany, NY: SUNY Press, 1981.

Savory, Theodore. The Art of Translation. Philadelphia: DuFour Editions, 1960.

Steiner, George. After Babel. New York: Oxford, 1975.

Vázquez-Ayora, Gerardo. Introducción a la traductología; curso básico de traducción. Washington: Georgetown University Press, 1977.

Walther, Rudolf, ed. Polytechnisches Wörterbuch, Deutsch–Englisch. Berlin: VEB Verlag Technik, 1979.

———. Wörterbuch der Technik, Englisch–Deutsch. Essen: Verlag W. Girardet, 1981.

Wilss, Wolfram. Are Training Programs for Translators Keeping up With the Times? Washington and Binghamton: National Resource Center for Translation and Interpretation, n.d.

———. Übersetzungswissenschaft: Probleme und Methoden. Stuttgart: Klett, 1977.

Woodsworth, Judith. "Training Translators in Canada: Theory and Practice." Proceedings of the 26th Annual Conference of the American Translators Association. Ed. Patricia E. Newman. Medford, NJ: Learned Information, Inc., 1985.

Symposium: Foreign Language Proficiency Criteria in Translation

COORDINATOR: GABRIELA MAHN;

CONTRIBUTORS: JERRY W. LARSON, JAMES R. CHILD,

PARDEE LOWE, JR., MARTHA HERZOG

One of the most complex challenges faced by translation educators is the evaluation of student translation skills. There are many factors to be considered in this evaluation of students. First, students' entry-level proficiency in both the source and target languages must be ascertained. Here we cannot be guided by oral or conversational competence in either language. We must test students' ability to comprehend the nuances of both languages. Second, in addition to linguistic competence this ability requires in turn knowledge of the cultures of the two languages involved, content knowledge or knowledge of a particular field, and general information. Third, translators are finally judged by how they express the message in the target language. Although programs vary in duration and intensity as well as in text types (e.g., literary, technical, legal, etc.), most programs find it advisable to evaluate students at set points during the course of study. Therefore, tests for different purposes and levels are necessary.

Little has been done on translation testing at the commercial or standardized level. Most institutions, whether governmental, educational, or private, design and administer their own tests.[1]

In foreign language education, the most discussed evaluation procedures of the 80's have been the *ACTFL/ETS Provisional Proficiency Guidelines*, based on language testing techniques developed originally by the Foreign Service Institute. The contributors to the symposium elaborate below on the history of proficiency testing. Since translator training is an integral part of foreign language education, it is inevitable that the discussion include the feasibility and desirability of applying some of these new developments in foreign language testing to translation testing. Accordingly, this series of articles explores the possibility of adapting foreign language proficiency criteria to the evaluation of students in translation programs: entry-level, progress points, completion and possible certification. Jerry W. Larson opens the discussion by establishing the distinctiveness of translation skills within foreign language proficiency skills. James R. Child presents the parameters of the proposed adaptation with a text typology. Pardee Lowe, Jr. sets up some testing models for translation. Finally, Martha Herzog shows how these testing methods are used by a government agency.

We believe that the contribution of specialists outside the immediate field of translator training is invaluable and invigorating. We wish to thank the contributors to this symposium for sharing their insights; we hope that considering translation skills testing has brought them new insights as well.

NOTE

1. Gabriela Mahn, "Towards a Model in Translation Training: Testing and Objectives," First North American Translators Congress (Fédération Internationale des Traducteurs), Training and Accreditation of Translators and Interpreters Section, Mexico City, February 28, 1986.

REFERENCE

ACTFL/ETS Provisional Proficiency Guidelines. Hastings-on-Hudson, NY 10706: ACTFL Materials Center, 1982.

Using the ACTFL Proficiency Guidelines to Assess Reading and Writing in Translation Programs

JERRY W. LARSON

With the current emphasis on the development of oral proficiency in most language programs, the skills of reading and writing usually do not receive a lot of attention. In translation programs, however, the emphasis shifts: reading and writing become the primary language skills. Not only do they receive the most attention, but a comparatively high level of proficiency in these skills is required of translation students.

The question has been asked whether it is appropriate in translation programs to follow the ACTFL Proficiency Guidelines for testing reading and writing. In pursuing an answer to this question, we should look at the various purposes for testing in a translation program, i.e., screening and admission, counseling and advisement, and end-of-program language proficiency certification.

Tests for Screening and Admissions

As mentioned above, the level of language proficiency required for translation majors is generally higher than that of majors in other language-oriented programs. Also, instead of placing stress on the improvement of language skills during their course of study, translation programs generally require their students to enter the major with sufficient reading and writing ability to enable them to pursue technical training without the language itself retarding their progress. In view of this requirement, it is essential to have some sort of measure that will aid in screening applicants, giving a reliable and universally understood ability or proficiency score.

Achievement test scores do not serve well as universal indicators of reading and writing ability, since they are not based on one standardized curriculum. Each institution has its own course requirements and grading criteria, meaning that an A, or a B, or 90%, or whatever achievement grade or rating that is reported at one school cannot necessarily be equated with the same rating at another institution. Because the ACTFL Proficiency Guidelines represent a standard or proficiency measure used nationally and are interpreted similarly by language educators across the country, it seems appropriate to use them for screening purposes.

Tests for Counseling and Advisement

On the other hand, if the purpose for testing is to identify particular language deficiencies so that counseling can be given, a global proficiency test, such as the ACTFL/ETS proficiency test, is not suitable. What is needed is a diagnostic examination that focuses on specific areas of knowledge and performance in the skills associated with reading and writing. A test of this type should be constructed so that it contains items dealing with all of the language-related concepts and information necessary for one to function as a qualified translator, including items assessing sensitivity to the target culture as well as knowledge of grammar principles, since a translator must be able to sense from the source language and convey to the target language similar feelings of excitement, disappointment, frustration, humor, and other cultural subtleties.

Tests for End-of-Program Language Proficiency Certification

The third purpose for testing is to certify the level of reading and writing proficiency of prospective graduates of the translation program. It is extremely important to be able to communicate to potential employers or other institutions a precise and meaningful assessment of a student's ability to perform reading and writing tasks commensurate with the demands of translation. As with tests for screening and admissions, this type of evaluation must be program- and curriculum-independent. Reading and writing proficiency tests similar to those outlined in the ACTFL Proficiency Guidelines would be appropriate, except for one major problem: the topmost rating on the ACTFL scale is Superior, which lumps together all performance from a level just above Advanced Plus to Native Speaker. Hence, these Guidelines simply are not sensitive enough to provide an accurate proficiency assessment for end-of-program proficiency certification.

Qualified professional translators often must function at a level far beyond an Advanced Plus ability level. The rating scale used to certify proficiency at this stage should be able to differentiate abilities at the upper end of the proficiency continuum. Either ACTFL will have to expand its rating categories, or the translation profession will have to settle on its own rating scale, perhaps adopting or adapting the ILR (Interagency Language Roundtable) numerical rating system, which does include additional discrimination among abilities at the upper end of the proficiency scale.

Language Proficiency and Translation

JAMES R. CHILD

Since the late 1950's the Government has used a set of proficiency descriptions covering four skills (speaking, writing, reading and listening) and six major points on a scale ranging from 0 (no competence) to 5 (competence of a native speaker). Five minor, or "plus" points are also identified giving a grand total of 11 possible ratings for a testee. These descriptions have been revised several times over the last 30 years (most recently in November 1983) and have proved serviceable not only to the Government but to the Academic community: the American Council on the Teaching of Foreign Languages (ACTFL) has used them as a model for developing a basically parallel set for Academia.

The wordings of both the Interagency Language Roundtable (ILR) descriptions (as the government statements are now called) and those of ACTFL are process oriented: they detail or at least imply what second-language learners can do in the course of demonstrating their various degrees of attainment in Oral Interview and other testing formats. However, it is clear that judgments on attainment are possible only when the judges have at hand criteria specifying at each level how native speakers/writers perform. In view of this, I wrote a paper in 1981 entitled "Language Levels and the Typology of Texts," in which I attempted to define from the source language point of view the linguistic elements to be mastered as they pertain to four levels of textual complexity.

The two approaches discussed above thus accommodate both the efforts of the learner of the target language and the performance of a native speaker/writer of that language. However, there is still no officially approved set of statements systematically calibrating the two, although several ILR members have pooled their talents to come up with some preliminary notions. Pardee Lowe identifies next in this symposium a number of factors involved in the translation process, over and above reading comprehension and writing ability in the receptor language (English for our purposes).[1] For example, Lowe points out the need to account for cultural differences, usually an obvious issue but sometimes involving subtleties below the surface. He also alludes to an "x factor" (which I term "congruity judgment") that is central to the translator's attempt to capture the full intent of the original passage. Congruity judgment which I discuss in somewhat more detail later is the attempt by the translator to capture in the receptor language not only the information structure but the style and tone of the original.

The important point, however, is that the translator must cope with all of these factors simultaneously in two systems (i.e., the source and the receptor languages). To do justice to this complex reality we need to develop profiles both of the translator and the texts he deals with. The difficulties in doing so are considerable, but I will offer some tentative ideas in making a start.

Texts, written or spoken, are the objects of the translation activity. In my paper on text typology mentioned above I presented a four-level system of classification from the simplest text type to the most complex and labelled them *orientational, instructive, evaluative,* and *projective,* respectively. While the restricted scope of this paper does not allow me to recapitulate the arguments supporting each textual type, I will point out that the first two levels (orientational and instructive) are concerned with specifying objects and facts describing events and situations, the latter two (evaluative and projective) with individual responses, cognitive and affective, to concrete phenomena. Most texts taken as wholes can be assigned to one level or another, but it is the rare text that can be described, for example, as a pure Level 2 or Level 4 passage: most are mixed.

Texts, too, are invariably "about something." This means of course that the translator must be able to read and write about those "somethings" with the requisite degree of authority. Questions of content, especially scientific or technical content, are of greatest interest at textual levels 2 through 4. Again, the compass of this paper is too restricted to do more than suggest the large variety of content problems a translator may face.

The notion of translation usually presupposes a source language text realized insofar as possible in the receptor language (occasionally a translator may have his reasons for not following this prescription). Because all texts are human products containing both cognitive and affective elements mediated by the cultures of which they are a part, they not only require context-sensitive interpretation but recreation in accordance with the requirements of the receptor culture. The higher the level, of course, the greater the demands on the translator. Similarly, the farther apart two language systems are—with system subsuming both formal and contentive elements—the greater the difficulty he will face, especially at the beginning of his work as a translator. At any textual level, low or high, there may be serious problems in translating where the two languages involved are vastly different in the ways they represent perceptions (of the physical world) not to speak of conceptions (of abstract entities). These phenomena have been thoroughly explored by scholars such as Benjamin Lee Whorf, Eugene Nida and a host of others.

As noted above, a basic assumption for developing translation skill statements is that the translator exercises several skills at one time (e.g., the ability to comprehend the source text in its own cultural terms; to write acceptably in his native language; to command the specialized knowledge a text may require). An equally important consideration is that the determination of his skill level be based on performance in accurately rendering source language texts, whose level of reading (listening) difficulty is known, as language texts at the same level.

To succeed in this task the translator must be able to operate in both languages at least one level higher than the object text or texts may require. It is only through such apparent "over-qualification" that the translator can make proper judgments on the line of demarcation between, say, the conveying of information tied in closely with the physical environment (Level 1 signs, announcements, etc., supported by an external frame of reference), and the reporting of information at some remove from the original impetus (Level 2 reports of happenings or descriptions of situations).

The real difficulties, however, emerge at Levels 3 and 4, because texts characteristic of these levels are "individuated." That is to say, they are no longer restricted to the basically social role of conveying or exchanging information, but are increasingly reflections of the inner cognitive and affective processes of the speaker or writer. Such texts, particularly belletristic products but frequently essays typical of the op-ed page of a major newspaper, may require close reading even though they are written in the native language of the reader. This is because content expectancy in general, and form expectancy in special cases such as poetry, may be so greatly reduced that the originator's intent becomes elusive. At these higher levels the translator must approach the competence of the native reader to "read between the lines" or "beyond the lines" (see the ILR descriptions of reading comprehension at Levels 3 and 4, respectively). Reading between and beyond the lines means of course that the translator is bringing to the text (as he often must do) meanings that are hinted at, or not made fully explicit in the original. Having drawn the appropriate inferences and acquired a global understanding of the text, the translator faces his toughest job: textual recreation.

Textual recreation or translation requires exercise of the "x factor" or "congruity judgment" mentioned earlier. Difficult to define, the concept addresses the need for the translator to judge his final product in its totality vis-à-vis the original. Since wholes are sums of parts, the translator must be aware of how the parts of the original text functioned in making up the whole so that he can preserve insofar as possible the whole-to-part relationship in the receptor language. Just as perceptions and conceptions are mapped differently from language to language, so discourses are organized in various ways. It is as if an artist working in water colors attempted to convey in that medium the intent expressed in an oil painting. While the very nature of the respective mediums, whether verbal or visual, resist total transfer, a reasonably able translator fully aware of the structural similarities and dissimilarities between the languages concerned can go a long way toward recreating textual values up to, say, low level 3. To capture the tone and stylistic turns of higher level texts, however, requires a considerable degree of intellectual and esthetic sensibility, beyond simple awareness of systemic differences between languages.

In summary, translator skill level statements must be tied to a system of description of increasingly complex textual types. In so doing they must specify for each skill level the simultaneous requirements of source language reading (listening) comprehension and receptor language writing skill; they must give due prominence to the issue of congruity judgment, according to the level described; and finally, they must exemplify through short extracts from material to be translated the variety of content, style, and tone inherent in texts at all levels.

NOTE

1. Listening comprehension and receptor language articulateness would be parallel criteria for the voice medium (i.e., in interpreting). Interpretation, however, entails elements beyond the scope of this paper.

REFERENCES

Brown, Gillian and George Yule. *Discourse Analysis.* Cambridge, MA: Cambridge University Press, 1983.

Child, James. "Language Proficiency Levels and the Typology of Texts," Georgetown University Roundtable Pre-Session, March 11, 1982. ACTFL publication forthcoming.

Interagency Language Roundtable Skill Level Descriptions. Arlington, VA, 1983.

Lowe, Pardee. "The ILR Proficiency Scale as a Synthesizing Research Principle: the View from the Mountain," *Foreign Language Proficiency in the Classroom and Beyond.* Hastings-on-Hudson, NY: ACTFL, 1985.

Nida, Eugene and Charles Taber. *The Theory and Practice of Translation.* Leiden, the Netherlands: E. J. Brill, 1974.

Revising the ACTFL/ETS Scales[1]
for a New Purpose:
Rating Skill in Translating

PARDEE LOWE, JR.

The Task

Translation is an intricate art. At its finest—reproducing in · one language the precise style and intent of an author writing in another—the translation skill comprises a complex of complicated tasks: an ability to comprehend the source language, including the ability to understand the author's style and intent, and an ability to render that style and intent accurately in the receptor language. Each language also possesses cultural and sociolinguistic aspects the translator must control. If the translation fails, one or more of these factors (possibly an identified, but as yet un-elaborated X-factor) may prove the culprit. This article discusses how the ACTFL/ETS scales reflect such factors and treats the scales' suitability in their current or possibly revised form for assessing proficiency in translating ability.[2]

As a result of the Presidential Commission's call for a "common yardstick," the American Council on the Teaching of Foreign Languages (ACTFL) completed Educational Testing Service's (ETS) pioneering work on the suitability of the ILR (Interagency Language Roundtable) scales for use in assessing language proficiency in Academia. Originally produced by the Department of State's Foreign Service Institute (FSI), the four government scales, one for each of the four skill modalities (Speaking, Listening, Reading, and Writing), have been subsequently refined by the ILR Testing Committee.[3] ETS and then ACTFL later modified the ILR scales. Two goals were paramount in their adaptation: first, commensurability was to be maintained with the parent scales; second, the resultant scales needed to be more sensitive to learner outcomes at the lower end of the ILR range. To achieve these ends, ETS and ACTFL subdivided the lower ILR levels into "low" and "mid," designating the ILR plus levels as "high." The ACTFL/ETS designation "Superior" subsumes all the ILR Levels above 3: i.e., 3, 3+, 4,

4+, and 5. Finally, ACTFL/ETS chose prose designations for the ILR levels, so that their "Novice" designates ILR 0; ACTFL/ETS "Intermediate" ILR 1; "ACTFL/ETS "Advanced" ILR 2. The resultant ACTFL/ETS scale contains nine levels plus a null point called "absolute zero," "no knowledge of the language."[4] Both the parent ILR and the derived ACTFL/ETS scales describe consistent and sustained proficiency (not sporadic achievement) in general language. Because the ILR and ACTFL/ETS scales have historically stressed *process over product*, a process orientation would be preserved in the modified scale suggested below.[5]

The suggestion that the ACTFL Guidelines might be applied to evaluate translation skill(s) is intriguing. The use of the ACTFL Guidelines as a starting point suggests that the resultant scale would characterize translating ability in "general language" rather than in some circumscribed "special purpose subject area" for which neither the ACTFL Guidelines nor their parent ILR scale prove suitable. ACTFL/ETS/ILR 'proficiency' by definition is "general language" ability.[6] Neither scale, however, was initially devised for rating translation skills, nor have they been subsequently employed to that end.[7] One reason may be that those assessing translation skills often focus on errors. Mistakes captured in black ink glaring at the rater from white paper tend to strengthen an error-centered approach, but for rating proficiency the ACTFL/ETS and their parent ILR scales address both patterns of strength and patterns of weakness in the assessment of the language user's performance.

A second reason for not using the ACTFL/ETS scales in their current form is their limited range, for government experience suggests that assessing translation requires characterizing the total ILR range. In their provisional form, the ACTFL Guidelines (1982) topped out at ILR Level 3. This upper limit poses a problem for rating translation, because ILR Level 4 proves to be the level in government experience at which users consistently tailor language to audiences and sustain a style level. In translation, tailoring language takes the form of matching source language style and intent in the receptor language. In the revised ACTFL Guidelines (1985) the limit for the *reception* skills (listening and reading) has been expanded to ILR Level 5. For these skills, the revised Guidelines at Superior and above describe the base levels (3, 4, 5), but lack the plus levels (3+, 4+). But the unexpanded ACTFL/ETS *production* scales only prove usable for rating a source language document rated up to and including Level 3. (The level of the source language document places a ceiling on the level that can be assigned the translation, since one would hesitate to state that a translator produced a Level Five translation based on a Level Four source document. Ideally, the two levels should match.) In contrast, the alteration in the ACTFL/ETS *reception* scales would presumably make them apply to rating the rendition from the source language document into the receptor language usable at Level 3 and higher. The missing plus levels, however, limit their utility. Perhaps, the ILR scales with their higher levels could be melded with the ACTFL/ETS subranges at the lower end to produce a combined ACTFL/ETS/ILR scale.

Coincident with the question of the number of levels required for rating translation is the question of whether the major contributing factors that the current scales address separately should remain in separate scales or be merged in a single composite scale. Neither the ACTFL/ETS nor the ILR scales currently contain *in one scale* such aspects as extent of comprehension in reading the source language and its varieties and styles along with its cultural, literary, and sociolinguistic allusions; ability to write the target language and to approximate source language features in the target language, etc. Hence, the question: should the relevant source language reading scale plus receptor language writing scale be used to confer a single global rating or to confer separate skill ratings?

Separate ratings possess the advantage of identifying which skill combination in which language proves the stronger: ability to read the source language or the ability to write in the receptor language. But using such scores still leaves un-rated several possible major contributing categories: sociolinguistics/culture, style, or the X-factor (that elusive quality which renders one translation clearly superior to others possessing equal ratings on the other factors enumerated here). These factors may to some extent already be reflected in the other scales, but may not be sufficiently elaborated to be employed in their current form to identify problem areas or to evaluate exit proficiency in a translation course sequence let alone for the assessment of developmental stages in the skill. Developmental stages reflect those milestones signalling the progressive gathering of the "bits and pieces" of language before they coalesce into a consistent and sustainable skill; for example, the passive acquisition of past tense forms in Germanic, Romance, and

Slavic languages at the Novice and Intermediate levels before having the consistent ability to recognize such forms with certainty and render them appropriately (generally a characteristic of the Advanced level). As yet no scale for style exists. And though a provisional ACTFL culture scale is available, the general consensus now suggests that more thought must be devoted to its form and content. One problem may be that culture, at least in government experience, appears to integrate automatically in a proficiency sense at Level 3 and higher, and yet in samples below Level 3 surfaces so sporadically as to be more readily testable as "achievement."[8] This phenomenon, in fact, parallels the style category which integrates even later—at Level 4 and up on the ILR scale. Needed for both categories (sociolinguistics/culture and style) in assessing their role in translation proficiency would be developmental ranges below these factors' respective integration points.[9] If all these factors were present, one could envision a profile of eight possible scores for a mythical candidate:[10]

Ms. T.R.A.N. Slator

1. Reading comprehension in the source language: _____
2. Writing ability in the receptor language: _____
3. Comprehension of style in the source language: _____
4. Control of style in the receptor language: _____
5. Comprehension of sociolinguistics/culture in the source language: _____
6. Control of sociolinguistics/culture in the receptor language: _____
7. Speed/Integrative ability: _____
8. The X-factor: _____

A global score might prove attractive if developmental stages need not be assessed. In such a case, two types of scores are possible: the first corresponding to a single verbal description of performance in the eight separately rated categories sketched above (but not derived additively from them)[11]; the second based on a single translation scale which incorporates those eight categories, but does not address them separately. To the extent that the major factors contributing to effective translation have been isolated and the nature of their contribution understood a separate translation scale would allow us to verbalize the unique gestalt, the special configuration of factors at each level which contributes to a single global score. Fortunately the ILR and

ACTFL/ETS have managed to date to describe the individual skill modalities rather successfully in a separate scale for each modality. Yet, a complex skill like translation would definitely challenge the Guideline writers. Rating a person's translation ability may prove easier in the deed than in trying to describe the translating process verbally, no matter how desirable the description of a single global score may prove. Moreover, if one desired to undertake remediation, such a lone global score proves a drawback for pinpointing the remedial area. A derived global score, on the other hand, which relies on ratings on the eight categories has an appeal, subject to all the caveats attendant upon the assigning of such scores in the parent ILR system.

In sum, translation proves to be an exceedingly complex skill. Some categories can be described by the ACTFL/ETS and ILR scales; other categories are insufficiently addressed by the scales. To use the ACTFL/ETS and ILR scales effectively for assessing translating ability the untreated categories must be described either in separate scales or in a composite scale, especially elaborated for rating translating ability. Can we bridge the gap?

The Plan

Doubtless many ways could be proposed to bridge this gap, to check whether an ACTFL/ETS/ILR scale might be modified for assessing the translation skill. Below we outline one possible proposal employing a composite scale, a proposal based on experience with developing and refining the ILR reading and writing scales.

1. Assign ILR Reading-levels to passages which have proven good predictors of suitable levels of comprehension and translation ability in the past. (The English passages graded by the ILR Testing Committee might provide a model.)

2. Assign ILR Writing-levels to approved translations of those passages. (If a single scale is desired, then a composite of these two scales at the same level could form the trunk onto which the comments cited in nos. 8–10 would be grafted.)

3. Select people as subjects representing a wide range of translation abilities to translate the passages.

4. Have expert translators rank the translations for each passage from

least to most successful and accurate. This ranking should proceed holistically based on patterns of both strength and of weakness.[12]

5. Have those modifying the scale attempt to rate these translations according to the ILR Writing-scale, at the same time gathering written comments on the differences in various translations of the same source language passage.

6. Compare the levels attained on the various translations to the ILR Writing scale.

7. Compare with each other translations from different source language passages, but rated at the same level.

8. Compare the comments assigned to translations rated at a base level, selecting those which prove common to a given ILR level for possible inclusion in either a separate category or a composite scale.

9. Devise verbal definitions for each base level of the translation skills, grounding the definitions on commonality – patterns of stength and of weakness, not quirk.

10. Examine the comments on those translations assigned plus levels, selecting suitable comments for inclusion in plus level descriptions, again basing the verbal descriptions on commonality. (If more distinctions are required at the lower levels the ACTFL/ETS scale could be combined with the ILR, to form the combined base scale.)

11. Field-test.

12. Review, revise, and finalize.

The Description Writers

To execute such a plan one could envision a committee whose members' overall approaches and general experience reflected the characteristics of the most successful proficiency description writers to date. These generally possess:

A. Ability to describe "gestalts," i.e., "wholes," not "parts"[13];

B. Ability to describe "process," not "product";

C. Ability to describe the continuous and sustained nature of ACTFL/ETS/ILR functions and the "threshold" nature of the system;

D. Ability to describe both "patterns of strength" and "patterns of weakness";

E. Extensive experience in one or more of the following:

1) translating expository prose in Academia;
2) translating expository prose in government;
3) translating special purpose prose (including literature) in Academia;
4) translating special purpose prose in government;
5) theory of translation with a balance in the actual practice of translation.

A Test

Finally, one can envision a technological breakthrough in translation test-taking itself: the candidate takes the test on a computer.[14] After signing on, the candidate reads the translation scale descriptions and chooses a suitable entry level. To aid the computer in selecting suitable passages the candidate will be directed to bracket her ability in the descriptions, selecting an obviously easy entry level for the first passage. When the candidate chooses an entry level, the computer presents her with a suitable passage in the upper half of the screen, leaving the lower half for the candidate to begin to write her translation. The computer will, subsequently, offer a medium passage and a hard passage. Having successfully tackled the three passage(s), the candidate could opt for progressively harder passages until she felt her skill has been adequately tested. If passages were to be timed, the computer would play timekeeper, alerting the candidate to the amount of time left for the level of passage chosen. At the end of the test, a knowledgeable translator/rater would call up the passage(s) and the candidate's translation(s), rate each globally, assigning the overall level which the candidate sustained most consistently according to the scale level descriptions. The computer screen could even split into thirds, offering the rater the original source language passage, the candidate's effort, and a model translation for comparison.[15] The rating completed, the rater could enter the data for statistical analysis and permanent storage as well as produce a certification form of the candidate's attainment.

Should one modify the ACTFL Guidelines to assess translation ability? Perhaps the idea can be transformed into reality—a scale which adequately characterizes translation skill across a wide range of levels that could serve as a basis for generating a computer-adaptive test of translation.

NOTES

1. *ACTFL Proficiency Guidelines, Generic and Language-Specific (French, German, Spanish)*. Hastings-on-Hudson, NY: ACTFL, 1982; *Provisional Language-Specific Guidelines in Chinese, Japanese, and Russian*, 1984; *Revised "Generics,"* 1985. The revised generics form the basis for the proposal suggested here. On the differences between the original "provisional" and current generics, see David V. Hiple, "A Progress Report on the ACTFL Proficiency Guidelines, 1982–1986," *Defining and Developing Proficiency: Guidelines, Implementations, and Concepts, ACTFL Foreign Language Education Series*, 17 (Lincolnwood, IL: National Textbook Co., in press).

2. The procedure suggested below could also apply to devising an "interpreting" scale, though the starting point, a composite scale, would derive from the ACTFL/ETS or ILR "Listening" and "Speaking" scales rather than from those for "Reading" and "Writing." A *composite scale* merges skill modalities across levels in the case of translation; say, Reading *plus* Writing. A *combined scale*, on the other hand, interweaves ACTFL/ETS subranges and ILR levels for a single skill modality, e.g., Speaking. Linked, the two scale types would yield a multi-skilled, multi-scaled system, a possible starting point for the proposal below.

3. *Interagency Language Roundtable (ILR) Skill Level Descriptions: Speaking, Listening, Reading, and Writing.* Washington, DC: ILR Testing Committee, November 1984.

4. *Strength through Wisdom: a Critique of U.S. Capability. A Report to the President from the President's Commission on Foreign Languages and International Studies.* Washington, D.C.: U.S. Government Printing Office, 1979; ETS, *Common Metric Project* (Princeton, NJ: ETS, 1979).

5. See Child's essay in this symposium as well as his forthcoming "Language Proficiency and the Typology of Texts."

6. See my "The ILR Proficiency Scale as a Synthesizing Research Principle," *Foreign Language Proficiency in the Classroom and Beyond*, ed. by Charles J. James, *ACTFL Foreign Language Education Series* (Lincolnwood, IL: National Textbook Co, 1985), 16: 9–53.

7. Judith E. Liskin-Gasparro, "The ACTFL Proficiency Guidelines: a Historical Perspective," *Teaching for Proficiency, the Organizing Principle*, ed. by Theodore V. Higgs, *ACTFL Foreign Language Education Series* (Lincolnwood, IL: National Textbook Co., 1984), 15: 11–42.

8. See note 6, *supra*.

9. Linda M. Crawford-Lange and Dale Lange, "Doing the Unthinkable in the Second-Language Classroom: A Process for the Integration of Language and Culture," *Teaching for Proficiency, supra*, pp. 139–177. Crawford-Lange and Lange suggest that the acquisition of culture is a process. In ILR experience, then, the process is being "set up" prior to Level 3 and some measure of "closure" is achieved at Level 3, with progressively greater "closure" from Level 3+ upwards.

10. See my " 'The' Question," *Foreign Language Annals*, 17 (September, 1984): 381 ff. These are the proceedings of the ACTFL Symposium on Receptive Language Skills, funded by the National Cryptological School, Defense Language Institute, Monterey, CA, November 1983.

11. On additive scores, see Ray T. Clifford, "FSI Factor Scores and Global Ratings," *Measuring Spoken Language Proficiency*, ed. by James R. Frith (Washington, DC: Georgetown University Press, 1980), pp. 27–30.

12. On "holistic rating," see Gertrude Conlan, "How the Essay in the College Board English Composition Test Is Scored" (Princeton, NJ: ETS, 1978) 8-page booklet. Also:

Mary E. Fowles, "Holistic Scoring: an Important Part of a School's Writing Program," *Interchange*, 5 (May, 1979): 1–6.
13. On "Gestalts," see note 4, *supra*, pp. 15 ff.
14. This approach is suggested in part by Michael Canale and contributors to the ACTFL Symposium on Receptive Language Skills (see note 10, *supra*). Canale's and David H. Wyatt's position papers appear in the sections entitled "Considerations in Testing of Reading and Listening Proficiency" and "Computer-Assisted Teaching and Testing of Reading and Listening," pp. 349–391 and 393–422, respectively.
15. Such an approach promises even greater utility for teaching translation skills.

REFERENCES

ACTFL. *The ACTFL Provisional Proficiency Guidelines, Generic and Language-Specific (French, German, Spanish)*. Hastings-on-Hudson, NY: ACTFL, 1982.
————. *Provisional Language-Specific Guidelines in Chinese, Japanese, and Russian*. 1984.
————. *Revised Generics*. 1985.
Conlan, Gertrude. *How the Essay in the College Board English Composition Test Is Scored*. Eight-page booklet. Princeton, NJ: ETS, 1978.
ETS. *Common Metric Project*. Princeton, NJ: ETS, 1979.
Fowles, Mary E. "Holistic Scoring: an Important Part of a School's Writing Program," *Interchange*, 5 (May, 1979): 1–6.
Frith, James R., ed. *Measuring Spoken Language Proficiency*. Washington, DC: Georgetown University Press, 1980.
Higgs, Theodore V., ed. *Teaching for Proficiency, the Organizing Principle*. ACTFL Foreign Language Education Series, 5. Lincolnwood, IL: National Textbook Co., 1984.
Hiple, David V. et al. *Defining and Developing Proficiency: Guidelines, Implementations, and Concepts*. ACTFL Foreign Language Education Series, 17. Lincolnwood, IL: National Textbook Co., in press.
ILR. *Interagency Language Roundtable Skill Level Descriptions: Speaking, Listening, Reading, and Writing*. Washington, DC: ILR Testing Committee, 1984.
James, Charles J., ed. *Foreign Language Proficiency in the Classroom and Beyond*. ACTFL Foreign Language Education Series, 16. Lincolnwood, IL: National Textbook Co., 1985.
Lowe, Pardee, Jr. " 'The' Question," *Foreign Language Annals* 17: 381 ff. (1984).
President's Commission on Foreign Languages and International Studies. *Strength Through Wisdom: A Critique of U.S. Capability*. Washington, DC: U.S. Government Printing Office, 1979.

Reading and Writing Tests at the Defense Language Institute Foreign Language Center

MARTHA HERZOG

The task of describing reading and writing tests at the Defense Language Institute Foreign Language Center has been greatly simplified by pairing this article with that of James R. Child. Child's work in this field has laid the foundation for DLIFLC's reading tests; his paper "Language Proficiency Levels and the Typology of Texts" should be studied by anyone attempting to test reading according to the government scale.

DLIFLC tests reading in three basic contexts – the evaluation of military language users for official purposes, the validation of these tests, and the testing of applicants for teaching positions.

Our tests for military personnel currently cover the range from Level 0+ through Level 3. While military requirements include comprehension of the strictly factual material found at Level 2 (Child's *instructive mode*), civilian translators will probably be concerned with texts at Level 3 and higher. Certain translators, I assume, concentrate on such text types as "news stories similar to wire service reports of international news items in major periodicals, routine correspondence, general reports, and technical material in his/her professional field."[1] The ILR descriptions explain that material of this type "may include hypothesis, argumentation, and supported opinions." However, Child emphasizes that these texts – exemplifying the *evaluative mode* – presuppose a certain amount of shared information between writer and reader.

Even more translators will probably work with texts at Level 4. Labeling this the *projective mode*, Child points out that these higher level texts presume little shared information. On the contrary the writer may display considerable originality of thought and style. Literature normally falls into this mode as well as certain types of technical papers and trail-blazing essays on virtually any topic. The innovative nature of this material would itself create a great demand for translation and transmittal to other cultures.

According to the ILR descriptions, the Level 4 reader understands "the full ramifications of texts as they are situated in the wider cultural, political, or social environment" and "the intent of writers' use of nuance and subtlety" and can "follow unpredictable turns of thought readily." Whether the text is evaluative or projective, it is imperative that its translator be fully capable of comprehending the content and intent. If the disparity between the reader's level and the textual level is too great, the reader may not even be aware that he has failed to comprehend the entire message. Presumably, formal programs train future translators to be skeptical of their reading proficiency and to use whatever means necessary to discover the writer's intent.

A reading comprehension test will tell the prospective translator and his teachers where he fits on the proficiency scale, which types of texts he can probably handle with full comprehension, and which types he should avoid until his proficiency improves.

When testing teacher applicants and when validating machine-scoreable tests, DLIFLC administers a face-to-face reading test. Two certified testers provide a series of authentic, graded texts to the examinee who must respond orally to several questions after reading each text at his own pace. The testers are prepared to be exhaustive in the number of levels tested, the variety of subject matter covered in texts at each level, and the extent of the questioning. The higher the examinee's level appears to be, the more care the testers must take that they test general reading proficiency and not special areas of competence.

DLIFLC cannot afford to test all of our graduating students in this tester-intensive manner; nor can we arrange face-to-face testing for the thousands of military personnel, assigned all over the world, who require regular re-evaluations. Therefore, we have had to design machine-scoreable reading tests that correlate highly with the thorough tests personally administered by a team of testers.

We use two formats that show strong potential for discriminating clearly between examinees with higher level reading proficiency.

The first is a variation on the cloze test that was developed by Child and his Defense Department colleagues. The rationale for deletions in this type of cloze depends largely on Hasan and Halliday's identification of cohesive features within a text.[2] At level 2+, texts are approximately 200 words in length with 40 deletions and an English paraphrase that provides all semantic information needed to understand the text. At level 3, the passages are 250 words long with 30 deletions and no paraphrase. Each deletion is numbered and marked with a symbol (triangle, star, etc.) that refers to a list of options. The examinee selects an option from the appropriate list and marks his choice on a machine-scoreable answer sheet. The objective is to restore the original text accurately.

The necessity that we machine-score the test and reuse the booklets creates relatively stringent conditions; examinees cannot write in their test booklets or make notes. If it were possible to restore the text directly by writing responses in the booklet, examinees would probably be more comfortable with this version of the cloze. We also believe this format is well suited for computerized testing.

However, even with DLIFLC's restrictions, results have been excellent. Typically, on tests using the cloze, the Kuder-Richardson 20 reliability coefficient has been .95, and the correlation with the face-to-face reading test has been .84.[3]

Table 1 shows the discriminating power of the cloze format at Levels 2, 2+, and 3; the solid line shows the results of the entire test.[4] The trend indicated by these response curves suggests that the cloze format would continue to discriminate well beyond Level 3.

Another promising format uses several complete passages, each about 200 words long, followed by questions and multiple-choice responses. While a few questions test only comprehension of concrete material, considerable effort is made to construct questions that test the reader's ability to connect ideas, read between the lines, and recognize the implications of the author's statements. Such questions are extremely difficult to write and require extensive experience with the level descriptions. In addition, this traditional multiple-choice format has a 25 percent chance factor, which must be offset by higher level texts than needed for the cloze with its negligible chance factor. Nevertheless, experienced testers can produce excellent tests of high level proficiency in this format.

Reliability of such tests has been .94, and the correlation with the external criterion has typically been between .85 and .90. Table 2 shows the discrimination power of the format.[5] Like the cloze, it shows potential for strong discrimination at higher levels.

Table 1

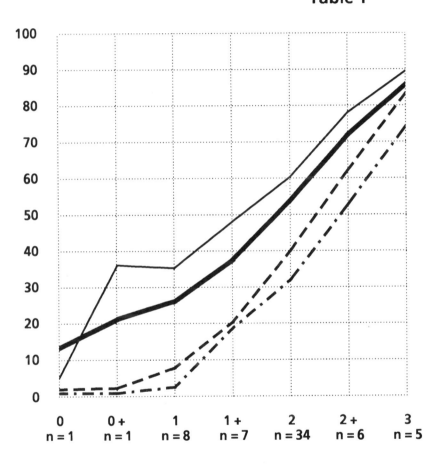

100
90
80
70
60
50
40
30
20
10
0

| 0 | 0 + | 1 | 1 + | 2 | 2 + | 3 |
| n = 1 | n = 1 | n = 8 | n = 7 | n = 34 | n = 6 | n = 5 |

cloze - Level 2
overall scores
cloze - Level 2 +
cloze - Level 3

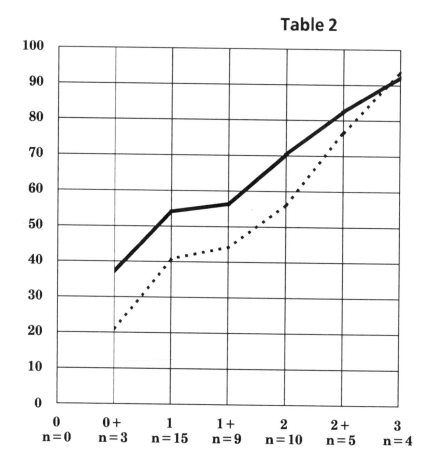

Table 2

Total ━━━━━━
Part IV ··········

At this time we only test the writing proficiency of prospective teachers, using a single essay. However, we intend to improve this test in the near future. Those familiar with the level descriptions for writing realize that a test measuring 3+ and above should require the examinee to produce material on more than one topic and in more than one style. In addition the examinees should demonstrate the ability to tailor material to a specific audience. Our revised writing test will be language-sensitive; topic, style, and assumed audience must represent target culture reality. While the proposed test will be lengthy and will have to be scored by trained testers, we do not believe there are shorter alternatives for measuring writing proficiency at the higher levels.

Although DLIFLC is only at the threshold of an adequate test of writing, our preliminary advice to those training translators would be to insist upon competence at the level of the original text. A higher level reader who lacks appropriate writing skills may be able to prepare reasonably accurate summaries of the text or to answer specific questions that interest his audience. But without the ability to replicate the author's presentation, to convey subtleties, or to address the audience with the style and tone of the originator, the translator will lose those qualities that make the text unique.

A multiple-essay test of the type DLIFLC proposes can determine whether the examinee is capable of writing at the desired level. In the long run, however, each translation itself is a test both of reading and writing.

NOTES

1. Quotations throughout are taken from the recently revised Interagency Language Roundtable (ILR) Language Skill Level Descriptions. Army Regulation 611-6, dated 16 October 1985, is the first of several government documents to publish the revised version.

2. M.A.K. Halliday and Ruqaiya Hasan, Cohesion in English (London: Longman, 1976). While the professional literature on cloze testing is extensive, an important article for cloze test developers is Lyle F. Bachman's "Performance on Cloze Tests with Fixed-Ratio and Rational Deletions," TESOL Quarterly 19 (3): 535–556.

3. The minimum acceptable reliability for DLIFLC's proficiency tests is .80; minimum criterion validity is .50.

4. Table 1 omits data from two other formats that discriminate well at lower levels. The entire test has five parts, three of them using cloze formats. The horizontal axis shows reading levels attained according to the ILR system; the vertical shows numerical

scores attained on the machine-scoreable proficiency test. Tables 1 and 2 were prepared by Sandra McIntyre of the DLIFLC Test and Standards Division staff.

5. The entire test has five parts. Table 2 shows only the format described and the test as a whole.

REFERENCES

Bachman, Lyle F. "Performance on Cloze Tests with Fixed-Ratio and Rational Deletions," *TESOL Quarterly* 19 (1985): 535–556.

Halliday, M.A.K. and Ruqaiya Hasan. *Cohesion in English*. London: Longman, 1976.

Establishing Project-Specific Criteria for Acceptability of Translations

MILDRED L. LARSON

Introduction

The goal of most translators is certainly to produce a translation which will be acceptable to the audience for whom it is being translated. This goal can only be achieved if the translator has a set of criteria which will guide him as he works and by which he can measure his final product. Such criteria will be different for different projects. The purpose of this paper is to suggest some of the matters which need to be considered in making decisions concerning the parameters of a given translation project.

Many translators have slaved long hours over a translation only to find that they couldn't find a publisher, or if their work was published, it didn't sell as they had dreamed it might. Before any translation is begun the question must be asked, "Who is going to read this translation? Is there an audience?" If it is clear that there is a readership, then the second question is "What are the characteristics of this possible audience that will affect the translation?" Once these characteristics are identified, the translator is ready to set up criteria, or guidelines, for the project.

Factors Which Affect the Translation Project

The characteristics of the audience which will affect the translation are very similar to those which affect the choices of any good writer. They include matters such as level of education, age group, occupation, previous knowledge of the subject, circumstances in which the text will be used, and more linguistic matters such as degree of bilingualism, dialect choice, and language attitudes. Each of these matters will be discussed below.

Level of Education. Is the translation for university people, the average person on the street, or new readers? If the sentences are long and the vocabulary rather technical, the average person will not put forth the effort needed to read the translation. On the other hand, if the form is too simple, more educated people might not want to read it. If the translator is hoping that the translation will be read by people with a wide range of educational backgrounds, then he will need to think about how to keep it from seeming too hard for some and too easy for others.

Age. If the source text and the receptor text are for the same age group, then age will not affect the form of the translation. However, sometimes it is desirable to translate for a different age group. For example, Kenneth Taylor, feeling that the then existing translations of the Bible were too difficult for children, produced the Living Bible Version. When he initiated his work his main criterion was 'age': it must be understood by young people.

The translation of Aboriginal legends into English in Australia is done with an adult audience in mind, usually anthropologists, and very technical language is often used. In the Aboriginal society, the legends are for adults and not considered children's stories. They do not, therefore, lend themselves to being translated into English for children to read without considerable adaptation.

Occupation. At first it may seem strange to mention the occupation of the target audience as an important factor in setting up criteria for a translation project. However, if the source text was written for lawyers and the translator is interested in selling his translation to a wider audience, he will need to be less technical than the original. Or if the source document is for medically trained people, it will need to be adapted for laymen.

Knowledge of the Subject. Perhaps one of the most difficult problems facing a translator is that of finding lexical equivalents for objects and events which are not known in the target culture. The lack of lexical equivalents may be due to difference in geography, customs, beliefs, worldview, level of technological development or similar factors. The original author and his audience had certain information in common which is not made explicit in the source text but may be essential to the understanding of the target audience. The translator will need to decide what kind of adjustments he will make along this line. Will he make such information explicit in the text itself or will he use supplementary material such as footnotes and glossaries? For example, a novel written 300 years ago in England would be based on the common knowledge of the author and audience about England—the geography, political situation, relationships with other countries at that time, etc. The author assumed this information. But the translator who translates that novel into Spanish for a Latin American audience today will find that his audience does not have this same background information. The translator will need to decide on guidelines for handling this difference.

Different Cultures. Unless the translator is really conscious of the cultural differences between the original audience and the new audience for whom he is translating, the result may be almost meaningless. A translator working in Surinam said that the language Alcance, spoken in the bush, is very similar to Sarangtongo spoken in the city. There is very little difference in the actual forms of the language. However, because the cultures are so different, they do not talk about things the same way. One is a city culture; one a bush culture. A translation of the "Tower of Babel" in the city was not understood by people in the bush because they didn't know the word used for "tower." It was not part of their culture so they had not learned it. All meaning is in some way culturally conditioned. The culture of the source text determined the meaning of that text. The culture of the target language speakers will affect how they understand the translation. The translator needs to decide how he will bridge the gap.

Circumstances of Use. The circumstance in which the translation will be used also affects the form of the translation. Is the translation to be used in oral communication or is it to be read by members of the target audience? In oral presentation the sentences cannot be long and complicated because the audience cannot go back and look again if they get confused. On the other hand, in oral presentations such as drama, the text can be supplemented with actions and thus made easier to follow. Only the printed word is available to the audience reading a text. Oral presentation does not allow for footnotes and other supplementary information which may occur with a text meant to used only for individual reading.

Degree of Bilingualism. The degree of bilingualism of the proposed readership may be an important issue for some translation projects. For example, if most of the people who will read the translation are bilingual in the source and target languages, then some key words may well be borrowed from the source language. If, however, the new audience does not know the source language, then great care will need to be taken in the selection of equivalents for key words.

When translating for an audience which is bilingual, the translator must also keep in mind that this will make it possible for the readership to compare the translation with the source text. Many people have a very narrow view of translation. They expect it to be literal, word-for-word. Or, even if they have a bit more tolerant attitude, they will be very critical if they find anything they consider "unfaithful" to the original. The translator has a bit more freedom of expression when he does not have this critical audience using the translation.

Language Attitudes. The success of a translation may also depend on the language attitudes of the desired audience. Is the language into which one wishes to translate considered the best vehicle for the material to be translated? For example, in Surinam the official language is Dutch. Sarangtongo is the trade language. In addition, there are several vernacular languages spoken there. Each language has a role in the society. Dutch is used when one is being formal or official. Sarangtongo is the language used when one is relaxing. A look at the bookstores makes it clear that a scientific book translated into Sarangtongo would probably not sell. In the bookstores all technical, educational, and scientific books are in Dutch. However, there are many books in Sarangtongo. They are books of poetry and novels. They speak to the "heart" not the "head." Knowledge about the role of the two languages will prevent a translator from putting a lot of effort into a translation which will not be accepted.

Variables in the Translation

An acceptable translation will need to vary to accommodate the factors discussed above. There are four principal variables—the choice of vocabulary, the grammatical structures used, the amount of implicit source language material which is made explicit in the target text, and the amount and type of supplementary material used. A translator will do well to consider the factors discussed in the previous section and the effect they will have on choices in these four areas.

Choice of Vocabulary. After the translator has his receptor audience clearly in mind, he is ready to set up guidelines for the type of vocabulary he will use. If he does not think about this in a definite manner, he is likely to end up with a translation which will seem inconsistent to the reader. Will he use technical words or only those used in common, everyday speech? Choices include formal versus informal, or even colloquial vocabulary. For example, would "ill," "sick," or "ailing" be the choice for this concept. For some languages a decision needs to be made as to level of politeness when deciding on the best word to use. This would be true for Japanese. There may need to be a decision made as to whether highly emotive vocabulary will be used or only words which are more neutral. For example, "irate" or "angry." These choices will depend on who the audience is and the purpose of the translation.

Choice of Grammatical Constructions. The same information can be conveyed by a variety of grammatical structures. Only after the translator has clearly defined his audience can he set up guidelines for choices on such matters as sentence length and complexity and types of grammatical constructions.

It is generally agreed that, in English, shorter sentences are used for material to be read by a person with a lower level of education and for children. Material prepared for a scientific audience is expected to have long, complicated sentences. The translator should set up general guidelines for sentence length based on the characteristics of the potential readership.

Certain grammatical constructions are easier to read than others. Different grammatical forms characterize different styles of writing. For example, in studying different texts we have found that in colloquial-type material the sentences are relatively simple with no more than two clauses connected by "and" or "but." In more technical material there are no complex noun phrases, prepositional phrases, or adverbial modifiers. Scientific language is difficult, not just because of long sentences but because of the use of many relative clauses. Depending on the characteristics of the audience for whom one is translating, a decision needs to be made concerning complexity and types of grammatical constructions.

Implicit Information to Be Made Explicit. The implicit information of the source text which will need to be made explicit in the translation will be significantly different for different audiences. The translator needs to decide before beginning the project whether he will add, in the text itself, the implicit information of the source text needed for an understanding of the target language. (See Larson 1984 for a fuller discussion.) How extensive these additions will need to be will depend again on the characteristics of the audience. How different is their background knowledge of the subject from the background knowledge of the original audience? How different are the cultural, social, or political situations of the source text audience and the target audience? Having looked carefully at the differences, the translator can set up goals concerning making implicit information explicit. For example, a translation of the Bible for a group in Africa which has had no contact with Christianity will need considerably more adjustment in the area of implicit to explicit information than will a translation for a group which has had a hundred years of Christianity. Because of more cultural commonality, the translation of a novel from German into French or English will probably not need as much adjustment as the same novel translated into an Asian language.

Use of Supplementary Material. The amount and kind of supplementary material that can be included with the translated text will again depend on the audience. For some audiences footnotes, glossaries, parenthetical statements, etc. are appropriate ways of handling the lack of correspondence in background and in implicit information. For other audiences this would not be the best way to communicate. The translator should decide early in the project if a glossary is to be included so that appropriate lists can be made from the very beginning. How many and what type of footnotes will be helpful to the target readership? These choices will depend on the level of education, occupation, age, etc. of this readership. A certain level of education is needed for footnotes to be used as a source of information to supplement the text and to provide the reader with background.

Checking the Criteria

The translator, on the basis of factors like those listed in the first part of this article, may choose a certain type of vocabulary, a general range of grammatical complexity and decide how implicit information will be handled. But he also needs to check to see if he is meeting his goal for communication. This is best done through comprehension checking. Translators tend to give their material to friends and colleagues who will smile and say, "It's great!" What is really needed is an effective way to be sure that the translation is communicating with speakers of the target audience.

The purpose of comprehension checking is to see if the translation is understood correctly by an unconditioned speaker of the target language. An unconditioned speaker is one who has not read the source text or the translation previously. It is important that such a person be a part of the audience for whom the translation is being prepared. If this person were highly educated, but most of the people using the material being translated have only a sixth grade education, the test would be invalid, because he might understand very well but the less educated who are to read the translation might not be able to understand the intended meaning. It is best to check the translation with persons from the real audience for whom one is translating.

Comprehension tests consist in having the unconditioned receptor language speaker retell back what he understood of the content of the translation and in his answering questions about it. The details of how this is to be done are included in the book *Meaning-Based Translation* (Larson 1984: 492–497). Questions may deal with content, theme, and style. Rountree (1985: 5) reports an experience in Surinam where she asked, "Was the person who told this story young or old?" The target language speaker said, "I think the person was old because a young person would not use these words. Only old people know those words." In another situation she got the response, "I think he was talking to children because the vocabulary is so simple." In another case, when asked about the person who wrote the text, the target speaker said, "I think he was in a hurry." Such a response would make the translator take another look at the translation to see why it left this impression.

The key to good checking is choosing people who represent the audience, that is, ones who have the characteristics identified in setting up the project. Loewen, consultant for the United Bible Societies in Africa suggests that:

Once a translator has identified the characteristics of his target audience, he should select, by name, four or five people who best typify this target audience. . . . Now the translator must learn to ask himself: "Does so-and-so understand this?" or "How would I say this if I were this moment speaking to him/her?" (Loewen 1985: 11–12)

And even beyond having the audience in mind, the translator needs to take the next step and actually check for comprehension with some members of this audience. Only then will he know if the guidelines he has established for the project are really effective or not. Only then will he be sure that the translation will be acceptable. The translation is most likely to be used if the translator first identifies the characteristics of the target audience, then sets up guidelines based on these characteristics, and finally checks the text itself with members of that specific audience.

REFERENCES

Barnwell, Katharine. "Testing the Translation," *The Bible Translator*, 28 (1975): 425–432.

Beekman, John and John Callow. *Translating the Word of God*. Grand Rapids, MI: Zondervan, 1974.

Headland, Thomas N. "Information Rate, Information Overload, and Communication Problems in the Casiguran Dumagat New Testament," *Notes on Translation* 83 (1981): 18–27.

Hohulin, E. Lou. "Readability and Linguistic Complexity in Translation," *Notes on Translation*, 91 (1982): 14–28.

Larson, Mildred L. "Traducción y Estructura Semántica," *Estudios filológicos*, 17 (1982): 7–21 (Valdivia: Universidad Austral de Chile).

————. *Meaning-Based Translation*. Lanham, MD: University Press of America, 1984.

Loewen, Jacob A. "For whom am I translating?" *Notes on Translation*, 107 (1985): 9–11.

Newmark, Peter. *Approaches to Translation*. Oxford: Pergamon Press, 1981.

Nida, Eugene A. and William D. Reyburn. *Meaning Across Cultures*. Maryknoll, NY: Orbis Books, 1981.

Reyburn, William D. "Cultural Equivalences and Non-equivalences in Translation," *The Bible Translator*, 20 (1969): 158–167.

Rountree, Catherine. "A Preliminary Guide to Comprehension Checking," *Notes on Translation*, 101 (1984).

Wonderly, William L. *Bible Translation for Popular Use*. London: United Bible Societies, 1968.

The Recruitment of Translators/Précis-Writers at the United Nations and Quality Control of Translations

FRANÇOISE CESTAC

I. INTRODUCTION

The Translation Division at Headquarters is part of the Department of Conference Services. It has a total of some 600 staff writers, 400 of whom are translators/précis-writers.

A. *Main functions of the Translation Division:*

(a) to provide translations of documents, official records, official correspondence and publications;

(b) to provide summary records of conferences and meetings as requested;

(c) to provide terminological services for United Nations translators and other users;

(d) to direct the training of translators and to co-ordinate their placement at Headquarters and at other duty stations.

B. *Structure of the Translation Division:*

1. Six Translation Services:
   Arabic Service
   Chinese Service
   English Service
   French Service
   Russian Service
   Spanish Service
2. A small German Translation Section.
3. A Documentation, Reference and Terminology Section.
Its functions are:
— to provide reference services for translators, interpreters and

editors, and to maintain specialized language collections for the purpose;
– to conduct terminological research to identify terminology appropriate to United Nations requirements;
– to issue terminology notes and to provide terminology guidance;
– to maintain a Translation Division Library in order to coordinate and centralize the language collections for the various Services/Sections of the Division.
4. A Contractual Translation Unit.
Its function is to provide a back-up operation for the Translation Services by arranging for some translation work to be done externally on a contractual basis.

II. RECRUITMENT OF TRANSLATORS/PRECIS-WRITERS.

A. *General Policy*
Translator posts are filled by candidates selected on the basis of competitive examinations in which staff members of the Secretariat as well as outside applicants may participate.

B. *Competitive Examination*
The purpose of the examination is to establish a list of qualified people from which vacancies in the Translation Division in the United Nations Secretariat in New York can be filled. Translators/précis-writers may subsequently be assigned to other duty stations in Africa, Asia, Europe, or Latin America.
1. Applications
Applicants must be graduates of a university or institution of equivalent status at which their main language is the language of instruction. They must have a perfect command of their main language. They must also have an excellent knowledge of English and of at least one of the other official languages of the United Nations, except in the case of applicants for the examination for English translators/précis-writers who must have an excellent knowledge of French and of one of the other official languages. The official languages of the United Nations are: Arabic, Chinese, English, French, Russian, and Spanish.
2. Written test
The written examination lasts two days. While the papers may vary according to the Secretariat's needs, the examination normally consists of the following papers:
(a) translation into the applicant's main language of an English text

of a general nature, except in the case of English translators/précis-writers who must translate a French text of a general nature (3 hours, approximately 700 words);

(b) summary in the applicant's main language of an English statement, except in the case of English translators/précis-writers who must summarize a French statement (2 hours, approximately 2,000 words);

(c) translation into the applicant's main language of two texts chosen from a total of five specialized English texts (economic, legal, scientific, technical, and social), except in the case of English translators/précis-writers who must translate two texts chosen from a total of five specialized French texts (3 hours, approximately 400 words for each text);

(d) translation into the applicant's main language of any two events chosen from eight texts offered in the other four official languages (i.e., other than the applicant's main language and the language of papers (a), (b), and (c) above), (2 hours, approximately 300 words for each text).

The use of dictionaries or other reference material is not permitted during the examination.

3. Oral examination and interview

Candidates who are successful in the written examination will be interviewed, normally ten to twelve weeks after the examination, by a Board of Examiners. The interview is an integral part of the examination.

The interview includes an oral examination, during which the candidate is asked to give an oral translation of a short English text (or in the case of English translators/précis-writers a short French text) after 30 minutes' preparation. A candidate who claims to know another language of interest to the Service concerned (either another official language of the Organization or a non-official language in the case of English translators/précis-writers) may be asked by the examiners to give an additional oral translation from that language.

The examiners then talk to the candidate in an endeavour to assess his or her general culture, career objectives, personality, ability to work in a team, knowledge of the United Nations, knowledge of reference and terminology work, readiness to accept revision and supervision, and willingness to serve at any duty station.

Candidates who are convoked to the interview are told not to assume that they will automatically be offered an appointment. The Board recommends the most suitable candidates for appointment. Its decision is final and is not subject to appeal.

C. Recruitment

1. Outside Recruitment

Translators/précis-writers are normally offered an initial two-year fixed-term appointment at the P-2 level. If those two initial years of service are satisfactorily completed, they may be promoted to the P-3 level and given a probationary appointment for a period of nine months to a maximum of two years. Upon completion of the probationary period, they are either given a permanent contract or separated from the Organization. Particularly competent translators/précis-writers may eventually be promoted to the P-4 level, as translators (self-revising) or revisers, and later on to the P-5 level, as senior revisers. Translators/précis-writers are expected to serve a minimum of five years in a language post and to serve at any duty station to which they may be assigned. Successful candidates may be expected during the course of their service to work on word-processing or similar data entry equipment for translation and terminological purposes.

2. Candidates selected from within the Secretariat

Staff members who are successful in the examinations for translators/précis-writers are assigned to the Translation Division for a period of two years with a special post allowance at the P-2 level.

At any time after completion of one year of assignment, staff members who are certified as having successfully qualified as translators are promoted to the P-3 level. The assignment may be extended for a further period not exceeding one year, upon completion of which the staff member may be promoted to the P-3 level. Unsuccessful staff members are reassigned to posts at their previous level, and the special post allowance is discontinued. Translators/précis-writers selected from within the Secretariat, like those recruited from outside, are expected to serve a minimum period of five years in a language post, and may eventually be promoted to the P-4 level and later on to the P-5 level, as senior revisers. They are also expected to serve at any duty station to which they may be assigned and may be required to work on word-processing or similar data entry equipment for translation and terminological purposes.

3. Recruitment of terminologists

Special mention should be made of this new category of linguists. The recent proliferation of international discussions on technical subjects requiring specialized vocabularies and the spread of EDP techniques for the management of terminological data have made the role of terminologists more important. Whereas in the past the need for terminological services was met by drawing on translation services, it has now become necessary to reassess the functions of the terminologists, with reference, *inter alia*, to linguistics and computerized information systems, and to consider the training and grading of terminologists at various levels with a view to standardization within the United Nations system. At the present time there are no recruitment examinations as such. The whole problem of the training and recruitment of terminologists is the subject of on-going discussions in various international bodies such as Termia and Infoterm and in universities which provide instruction in this discipline.

III. ON-THE-JOB TRAINING

The duties of translators/précis-writers are

(a) to translate into their main language from any of the other official languages, but occasionally also from other languages, documents relating to various aspects of United Nations activities: political debates, economic, social and legal reports, international agreements, scientific and technical studies, and official correspondence;

(b) in the case of English, French, and Spanish translators/précis-writers, to attend meetings of United Nations bodies and draft summary records of their proceedings.

While the various Translation Services have different needs and follow different approaches to training, they all have on-the-job training programs, carried out under the supervision of a Training Officer (a post held by a senior reviser at the P–5 level).

The Training Officers of the various Services meet periodically with the Director of the Division for an exchange of views and experiences, in the course of which each Training Officer describes the problems encountered in his or her Service and the methods used to deal with those problems. They thus learn from each other's experience.

Soon after they join the Translation Division, trainees are taken to visit the main units of the Department to become acquainted with their work and responsibilities.

As regards the training process itself, it must be emphasized that a strong training program has been found to be indispensable as relatively few recruits have had any formal training as translators and some may not even have any experience of translation work, let alone United Nations work with its highly specific requirements.

Experience has shown that trainee translators are best trained individually and, as far as possible, on the job. Newcomers therefore receive systematic guidance during their first two years. Upon arrival, they are given a series of briefings by the Training Officer, who explains how the Service operates, describes methods of work and recommends background reading material. They are also provided with a set of written instructions which incorporate the basic rules and guidelines to be followed and which are designed to facilitate the work of the translators. Each Service maintains its own set of instructions.

The first translations done by a trainee translator are revised by the Training Officer, who then discusses with the staff member any corrections and changes made and offers advice and suggestions on ways to improve the quality of the work. The Training Officer thereafter keeps in close touch with the new staff member, giving advice before, during, and after the translation of each job as long as necessary. The Training Officer is assisted by the revisers, who are also expected to offer guidance and, if deserved, encouragement to the new translator in the light of the individual jobs they revise.

Throughout their first two years, trainees are kept informed of their progress by the Training Officer who, having gone over the revised drafts of their translations and having discussed their work with the revisers, is able to evaluate their overall performance. Even more importantly, they receive their corrected drafts which, whenever necessary and possible, are discussed with them by the Training Officer and the revisers concerned.

A reviser who revises a job done by a trainee is also urged to fill in an evaluation sheet relating to that particular job. The evaluation is given to the Training Officer who discusses it with the trainee, along with his or her own comments if need be.

In the English, French, and Spanish Services, where translators are also expected to serve as précis-writers, trainees undergo separate training in précis-writing. The trainees are given a briefing by the Training Officer on the various aspects of the task they will be called upon to perform. These briefings are followed by practical exercises, or "dry runs," in which trainees are sent into meetings to take notes and then write up a mock summary which is reviewed and commented upon by the Training Officer. Such practical exercises are repeated until the

Training Officer feels that the trainee understands what is required of him or her, seems capable of doing it reasonably well, and can therefore be assigned to a précis-writing team.

The training process, both in translation and in précis-writing, is of course more or less intense according to the individual: some trainees merely require a few promptings to be put on the right track, while others need to be closely monitored throughout their training period. In any case, it should be noted that training cannot compensate for a lack of talent, nor can it be a substitute for the personal effort needed to build up an extensive body of knowledge and to acquire a firmer command both of the linguistic tools and of the issues dealt with at the United Nations. In this effort, the trainees are helped by means of the feedback they receive on their work through their discussions with the Training Officer and the revisers, and through a study of the revised drafts of their translations, which are returned to them so that they may learn from the corrections made by the revisers. The importance of this personal effort by the trainees and of their contribution to their own improvement cannot be over-emphasized, for, while the new recruits can, through training, be helped to work more efficiently, they cannot be taught those basic qualities that are essential to a good translator—a perfect command of the target language, a good general background, an ability to learn and broaden one's knowledge, and, above all, sound judgment.

The obvious aim of training is to improve the quality of the work, as well as to enhance the efficiency of the Service as a whole. However, time spent on training—on the part of the Training Officer, the revisers, and the trainees themselves—is time taken away from production. A proper balance must therefore be found when devising a training program, for it should be borne in mind that Translation Services are production units, not translation schools, and that there is a limit to the time and effort that can and should be devoted to training.

Finally it should be pointed out that the training process described above which, in the case of new translators, takes place in a very systematic way, does not stop at the end of the two-year training period. It is a continuing process, although on a less systematic basis, since even fully-fledged translators are expected to study the revised drafts of their translations and revisers are expected to offer advice and suggestions to the translators and to fill in evaluation sheets relating to jobs which, in their opinion, deserve special comment.

IV. QUALITY CONTROL OF TRANSLATIONS

After having reviewed the procedures for the recruitment of translators/précis-writers, on the one hand, and their on-the-job training, on the other, let us now turn to the issue of performance, in particular the quality control of translations.

A. *Revision and self-revision*

As already stated, the primary function of the Translation Division is to provide translations into the official languages of the United Nations – and into German – from the official languages and from a number of non-official languages, of documents, official records, official correspondence and publications. Translation is here used as a generic term, although it also includes revision and/or self-revision, the latter concept having been introduced some years ago to enhance the career prospects of translators and improve the efficiency of the translation process. "Revision" can be defined as the verification or correction of translations by another, generally more experienced, translator. "Self-revision" can be defined as the verification or correction of his or her own translations by the translator.

Although it is difficult to lay down rigid rules as to who should translate and/or revise what types of documents, self-revision is generally performed at the P–4 level, and in some cases at the P–3 level, while extremely important or difficult documents are often assigned to P–5 senior revisers.

A clear distinction must be established between the types of documents which are suitable for self-revision and those which require revision. Documents which are suitable for self-revision include ephemeral documents, routine correspondence, summary record translation, and short easy documents.

Documents which require revision include legal texts (including treaties), draft resolutions, sensitive political documents, original summary records, and the work of junior translators, as well as jobs done by more than one translator which require revision for the purpose of ensuring consistency.

The distinctions between a reviser, a self-reviser, and a translator are often blurred. Translators have different degrees of experience: some of them are so inexperienced that they are involved only in translation subject to revision; others are capable of putting out at least some of their own work with very little supervision; some of the latter may be able to revise work done by other people; and still others are so experienced that they are used almost exclusively for quality control (that is, revision or other forms of monitoring) and administration (including training, programming, and terminological research). Revision is an internal stage of translation and, like terminological research, is very important for quality control. Without proper lexicons, the process of translation is slowed down. Without revision, when it is required, the gain in translation time is offset by a loss of quality.

Self-revision, in the case of suitable jobs, can enhance job satisfaction for the translators without a noticeable loss in quality. Revision will, however, always remain the essential factor in quality control.

B. *Other factors inherent in quality control*

Although quality control is primarily the responsibility of translators (used here in the general sense to include translators, self-revisers, and revisers), there are other functions within the translation process which contribute to quality control.

1. Reference and terminology

These functions provide support services for the Translation Services. Before a job is sent for translation, reference clerks scrutinize sources, trace quotations and titles, and indicate any parts of the text which have previously been translated. They identify material which provides the historical context and useful background. Once the translator has received the referenced document, his or her work is further facilitated by the availability of authenticated terminological data extracted from specialized and other publications by the terminologists.

2. Pre-editing

Pre-editing is essential in many cases to ensure quality control of the texts submitted for translation. Some texts are poorly presented, some are virtually illegible, expecially some of those submitted in languages with a non-roman alphabet, and some present problems of grammar or syntax, particularly those written in a language which is not the author's main language.

3. Programming

This can be defined as the task of adapting the volume and flow of the material received for translation to the manpower resources available to the Translation Services at any particular time with a view to completing the translations within the specified deadlines.

Documents vary not only in size, but also in subject matter and degree of difficulty and sensitivity.

They should whenever possible be assigned to translators, self-revisers, or revisers who possess the necessary expertise in the field in order to maintain high standards of quality in translation and to increase productivity by reducing the time devoted to research. Unfortunately, it is not always possible to assign work to someone with the necessary expertise. The number of fields covered by United Nations documents is so large that no Translation Service, however well staffed, can be expected to have a sufficient number of experts in all areas. The next solution is to assign the work to those staff who are most likely to have a workable knowledge in the particular field, or those who are deemed to have the ability to undertake the necessary research to produce an acceptable translation on the subject in question, and leave the polishing to the reviser. Considerations of quality, however, require that under these circumstances a final coordinator should read through the document in its entirety with a view to ensuring the necessary uniformity of terminology and consistency of style.

Thus, apart from simple availability of the necessary member of the staff at any given time, there is the no less important question of the composition of the staff, namely, the ratio of experts to generalists; the ratio of trainees, or relatively inexperienced, staff to the relatively experienced; and the number of fields covered by experts. Not only are there wide differences among the various Services in all these areas, but the same Service may show markedly wide differences in the ratios in question at different times.

4. Feedback from users

It is essential that Translation Services receive feedback from their users, including submitting departments and delegations, especially when texts are of a very difficult or a sensitive political nature.

V. CONCLUSION

Thus, to sum up, high standards in the recruitment of translators, rigorous on-the-job training, and constant quality control are considered equally essential to an efficient translation operation and are the three major goals of the Translation Division at United Nations Headquarters.

Recruitment and Retention of Staff and Freelance Translators: Experience at One International Agency

The World Bank—or, to give it its full title, the International Bank for Reconstruction and Development (IBRD)—is hardly typical of the genus "international organization": it does not have seven or eight official languages, and in fact it does not even have an official language. English is, however, for all practical purposes, the Bank's "working language." Despite the absence of formal multilingualism, the realities of a polyglot world require translation and interpretation from and into English for many aspects of the organization's work.

Founded 41 years ago in 1945, as one of the two "Bretton Woods institutions" (the other being the International Monetary Fund or IMF), the World Bank's business is to help developing countries grow economically and improve standards of living by providing technical advice and lending money for sound development projects (e.g., dams, roads, irrigation schemes). More recently, the Bank has also been making program loans and "structural adjustment loans" designed to help the developing countries implement economic reforms. Affiliated with the World Bank are the International Development Association (IDA), which lends to the poorest of the developing countries on "concessional" terms, and the International Finance Corporation (IFC), which supports development of the private sector in developing countries. For convenience, I shall use the term "World Bank" to refer to all three institutions. The World Bank is located in Washington, D.C., as is the International Monetary Fund.

Translation and interpretation services for the World Bank are provided by Language Services Division (LSD), which is attached to Administrative Services Department (ADM). LSD itself is subdivided into a number of sections or units, each headed by a "program manager."

To understand LSD's internal structure, it is necessary to retrace the growth of our various language programs. The first few translators were hired to translate texts from French, Spanish, German, and other European languages into English for informational and operational purposes; then, in the early 60's, the newly independent former French colonies needed to have documentation sent to them in French; Spanish was added a little later for Spain and most of Latin America; the oil shocks of the 70's greatly increased the need for translation to and from Arabic; and about five years ago the People's Republic of China rejoined the Bank, giving rise to a considerable amount of English to Chinese and Chinese to English translations. The language combinations mentioned are handled "in-house," capacity permitting. Excess demand, and requests for other language combinations (such as translation to or from Thai or Turkish or Nepali) are handled by freelance contractors. There is also a small interpretation section, with four interpreters providing simultaneous and consecutive interpretation in English, French, and Spanish, supplemented where necessary by freelances for other combinations.

LSD has a total staff of 88, of whom 44 are translators and the remainder support and front office staff. The ratio of translators to total professional staff in the World Bank (44:3,142 or 1.4%) is extremely low in comparison with other international organizations, where it generally lies in the 10–20% range. Not surprisingly, therefore, the World Bank also has one of the highest contract ratios (about 50% of total workload in all language combinations).

Recruitment of new staff translators is a relatively rare occurrence, not only because staff numbers are small but also because staff retention is generally high. The average length of service of World Bank translators currently stands at more than ten years. This stability obviously produces a dividend in terms of institutional memory and familiarity with procedures and specialized terminology. The staff translator, to give just two examples, will know that IBRD makes "loans" but IDA grants "credits," and also that "évaluation d'un projet" is rendered in English as "project appraisal," while the English term "project evaluation" must be put into French as "évaluation rétrospective d'un projet."

However, two to four vacancies have to be filled each year. The skills required—in addition to extensive prior experience in translation—are degrees in languages, diplomas in translation, and/or substantive qualifications in such fields as economics, law, accounting, etc. Except for the Arabic and Chinese translators, who work both to and from English, all staff translators work exclusively into their mother tongue. English translators are required to work regularly from French, Spanish, and Portuguese; knowledge of German, Dutch, Italian, etc. confers added flexibility in handling the section's workload. French and Spanish translators are required to work only out of English. Recruitment is by competitive written examination (held in Washington, London, Paris, or other major cities), evaluation of test papers (coded to ensure anonymity), and personal interviews. As a general rule, translators are hired in mid-career after several years of experience in the profession, preferably in other international organizations.

Given the World Bank's preference for recruiting staff in mid-career, schools of interpretation and translation are not primary sources of recruitment. Because of the small size of the Bank's translation staff, it is not possible to run a trainee or *stagiaire* program. Experience has shown that advertisements in leading newspapers and journals (e.g., *Le Monde, The Economist* and such publications as *La Nación, El Mercurio,* and *El País* in Argentina, Chile, and Spain, respectively) produce the best response; recommendations can, of course, also be obtained from schools of translation regarding graduates who have now gained sufficient experience in the profession. Occasionally, worthwhile candidates who have recently arrived in Washington approach LSD spontaneously; word-of-mouth contacts can also be very important. As recruitment is generally on a "one-off" basis, examinations are as a rule held to fill a specific vacancy, not to establish a waiting list, as is the practice in some larger organizations.

As indicated earlier, the average World Bank translator has more than ten years' Bank service. This stability can be attributed in part to attractive working conditions, but probably even more to the nature of the work. Virtually everything we translate is operations-oriented, i.e., designed for immediate action, rather than for the files (an unfortunately frequent side-effect of a formal policy of multilingualism). We also are called upon to handle an immense range of subjects (the World Bank's activities could be said to embrace every aspect of human endeavor except for sports and military matters). To give an example, the writer recently handled reports on town planning in Brazil, cardboard manufacture in Yugoslavia and telecommunications development in Laos. The Arabic Unit, for its part, recently translated a research paper on *qat*, the East African narcotic. The French and Spanish Sections have translated detailed descriptions of contraceptive methods and practices as part of an in-depth study of the effects of the population explosion on development. This kind of diversity presents a continuing intellectual challenge and contributes to a high level of "job satisfaction."

As is generally the case in the profession, career growth is limited. Although most staff are recruited at the Translator level, some with only limited experience have been recruited as Junior Translators. After a number of years of satisfactory performance (the first year is in any event a "probation" year), Junior Translators may be promoted to the rank of Translator, and Translators may be promoted to Senior Translator or to Translator/Reviser. The work of Senior Translators is "self-revised," i.e., they themselves accept full responsibility for its accuracy, completeness and appropriateness of style. Translator/Revisers "revise" (i.e., edit and correct where necessary) the work of less experienced colleagues and, in addition, produce final translations on their own responsibility. Translators (and Junior Translators) receive on-the-job training from one or more experienced revisers, in the form of direct feedback on their draft translations. Promotion is preceded by a trial period during which the (Junior) Translator's ability to function at the higher level and produce translations of dependable quality is carefully assessed. A range of training courses on multiple aspects of the World Bank's operations (e.g., Economics for Non-Economists, Basic Accounting, and Finance) are regularly offered to Bank staff, including those in LSD. Further internal support is offered by a specialized Library and Reference Unit (with over 10,000 dictionaries, glossaries, handbooks, and other printed materials), and a Terminology Unit, which has produced printed glossaries of specialized terms and is currently introducing an automated terminology entry and lookup system which all the translators who have opted to have a Wang WP terminal will be able to access directly.

As indicated earlier, a very high percentage (roughly 50%) of the World Bank's translation volume is handled by contractors. Where demand is too small or too "lumpy" to justify a staff position (e.g., the amount of translation from English to German would barely amount to a month's work spread over the entire year), it makes sense to develop a roster of qualified professionals to take on such assignments when they do come up. Despite the relatively favorable situation in Washington, with its diplomatic community, several universities, and half a dozen international organizations, there can be real problems in finding a qualified freelance translator when you need one. Recently, a translation from Maltese to English (fortunately not a rush job) had to wait for a month until our only known translator returned from vacation in Europe!

To administer its extensive contract operations— roughly 1,600 jobs a year out of a total of 4,600 requests a year in the various language combinations—LSD has set up a Contract Office to maintain an up-to-date roster of freelances available in Washington and other cities in a dozen countries, ensure that jobs are placed with the best people available at any given time, track jobs to make sure they are returned on or before the due date, and handle payments.

Where predictable peaks in demand occur, as with the early-summer rush to translate the Bank's Annual Report and the yearly World Development Report into French and Spanish, short-term "consultants" are taken on board to help LSD complete these assignments on time. These "consultants" are typically retired translators who formerly worked for other international agencies.

The language combination that gives us the greatest problem is English to French. The number of qualified freelances in the Washington area falls far short of demand. As a result, whenever time permits, some freelance assignments have to be placed in Geneva or Paris. At the moment, this adds 1-2 weeks to total turnaround time; but facsimile transmission and courier services promise relief here. Because of this chronic dearth of good French translators, the French Section also differs from the other sections in holding examinations for potential freelances and creating a "pipeline" of potential candidates for consultant or staff positions.

Freelance translators working into languages other than English generally suffer from the disadvantage of being at a remove from their linguistic base. But when working on an assignment for LSD, they will normally be able to consult the author of the original text (unless he or she happens to be away on mission) when they feel this is necessary. Staff and freelance translators working into English, however, seldom have the opportunity to discuss obscure points with their authors, as the writers are likely to be stationed in Paraguay or Zaire, for example. When time allows, the work of freelances is revised or reviewed, and feedback is provided, to improve the quality of future assignments.

What qualities do we demand in a potential freelance translator? There are three basic qualities every translation service looks for: timeliness, accuracy, and style. If a job is needed by Tuesday 10 AM, it must be there by 9:59 AM at the latest. If the Contract Officer has to make six anguished phone calls to get the translator to produce the job by 3 PM the following Friday, you can be sure that, even if we do pay for the job, such an unreliable contractor is unlikely to hear from us again. The translated text must be a complete and accurate version of the original (no paragraphs or sentences may be omitted, proper names and figures must be correctly reproduced, the information contained in the text must not be distorted in any way, and specialized technical terms must be precisely rendered). And, last but not least, the style of the translation must be appropriate to the nature of the text and the time allowed for its production (e.g., no jarring foreign turns of phrase, no high-flown language in a basic technical report, no colloquialisms in the translation of a foreign law).

The issue of style is one that is likely to receive a lot of attention in coming years, as machine translation systems are increasingly used to produce texts for "information purposes only." The "inaccurate" translator and the "tardy" translator will find themselves pushed out of the market, while those with a sure sense of style will find their talents in greater demand, whether as posteditors or as translators of highly demanding texts.

Languages in the Federal Government

ALICE OTIS WITH TED CRUMP

Excellence in translation is of considerable concern in the Federal Government, where translation often embraces a wide range of functions demanding linguistic facility and extensive subject knowledge and where prudence as well as accuracy may be essential to the national image in the fields of diplomacy, politics, science. In some agencies, the attempt to achieve highest quality in the shortest time and at least cost is complicated by the need to work with many languages, often esoteric, and with peaks and valleys of demand that cannot be predicted. The variety of tasks to be performed may be one of the factors that influence one agency's preference for staff rather than contract translators, while, on the other hand, large quantities of non-sensitive translations in many language and technical areas favors another agency's greater use of contractors.

Concern with excellence is reflected in testing and monitoring of contractors, in requirements for employment, in editing and reviewing procedures, in the opportunities offered staff members to improve their skills, adapt to new technical aids such as word processors and machine translation, and expand subject knowledge and in the career opportunities available in some agencies. This article is based on Ted Crump's *Translation in the Federal Government: 1985* which provides detailed figures and information for those who may feel that their talents can assist the Federal Government in meeting the challenge of achieving excellence in translation.

Some government translators, those at the State Department and the Federal Bureau of Investigation (FBI), for example, may find both constant challenge and interesting variety in the material they translate; others may have diverse duties. Translators provide interpreting services at the Naval Intelligence Support Center (NISC), the Congressional Research Service of the Library of Congress (CRS), and the National Institutes of Health (NIH), with CRS translators assisting with international phone calls in Congressional offices. Oral translations are frequent at the United States Patent and Trademark Office; they are sometimes used at NIH to determine whether there is a need for a written translation, and at the Technical Translation Division at Wright-Patterson Air Force Base for fast translations of short articles and evaluation of books.

CRS translators cover a wide range of subject matter—from sciences, such as biology and geography, to narcotics, politics, and the liberal arts—in the form of letters, speeches, articles, and other documents sent by Congressmen. Reports, letters, and articles are translated at NIH too, but the subject matter is concentrated in the biomedical area and therefore requires considerable technical expertise. Science and technology are not the only subjects translated by the staff of the U.S. Army Foreign Science and Technology Center (FSTC), nor are their duties confined to translation. The FBI employs a large number of translators who analyze and summarize diverse materials. Abstracting is performed along with translation by language specialists of another arm of the Library of Congress, the Federal Research Division (FRD). The translation staff at Wright-Patterson Air Force Base, all hired as "human translators," have been on the job long enough to experience a great change in their duties. "Of the 11 translators 3 do human translation and the rest develop systems or do post-editing of machine translation (MT)" (25). MT is said to produce 30% more than human translation. Whether the 11 or the 3 receive oral translation assignments was not stated. A job announcement circulated by the Defense Mapping Agency (DMA) describes a highly challenging translator position requiring translation of "the most difficult technical and scientific material from Russian and Polish and/or Czech into English for subject matter experts," as well as reviewing and editing machine translations, analyzing and abstracting technical material, and reviewing and editing contract translations. The announcement stresses "readability, accuracy," "proper phrasing, syntactical structure" (36). Resourcefulness will be essential for this job along with translating and technical skills, since the work involves terms for which no equivalents are known.

Versatility is needed at the Department of the Interior, where the sole translator must arrange for and test contractors for 80 to 90%

of the translations she processes and review the contracted translations. Although she translates five languages, fourteen are handled
regularly through the office. Translation is done largely by employees
of lower grade levels at the Bureau of the Census, where there is an
emphasis on statistics and programming. Here and at the Social Security
Administration (SSA) there are forms to be translated, although SSA's
interest is in extracting pertinent data that appears on documents rather
than in the forms themselves. The Voice of America (VOA) no longer
hires translators as such but International Radio Broadcasters, who
"have a quadruple function – translate, adapt to the target audience,
write the script, get on the air and deliver it" (17) and may also perform simultaneous interpretation.

Scanning, abstracting, and analyzing are performed by language
specialists at the National Security Agency (NSA), FRD, and the Central Intelligence Agency's (CIA) Foreign Broadcast Information Service (FBIS), which monitors a variety of media and sends selected
printed materials to the Joint Publications Research Service (JPRS),
also a branch of CIA, for translation. In-house JPRS translators do
not translate; they review and edit the work of outside translators.
CRS has analyzed films for Congressmen; it also provides information, which may involve research projects, and transcribes tapes.
Transcription is performed at NSA and the FBI, where wiretaps can
provide a difficult task.

Teaching, tutoring, and testing are other duties of language personnel. CRS translators are called upon to tutor members of Congress
who want to improve their pronunciation of foreign languages; experienced NISC linguists may teach languages and translation to reser-
vists; FBI specialists test applicants' foreign language skills by phone.
At NSA, in addition to teaching, staff members prepare language-
related materials – glossaries, grammars, courses.

The problem of weighing quality against quantity emerges in the
varied and changing quotas set by some agencies. The State Department lowered its expected volume from 2,000 words a day to 1,600
with a weighting factor to consider difficulty of translation. NISC ex-
pects a rate of 1,200 words a day in edited draft form, or half that
number for Asian languages. The Patent Office works on a scale that
considers 150 to 180 words per hour (statistically 840–1,440 words a
day) satisfactory for a non-Japanese primary language, with more than
180 rated as outstanding and lower expectations for a secondary

language. SSA anticipates an output of 3,000 words a day from an experienced translator. This seems to reflect the fact that many documents are involved; therefore, there is repetition and few, if any grammatical structure or idiom difficulties to be resolved. At NIH a "Fully Met" quota is one of 125–190 words an hour, both written and oral (1,025–1,520 in eight hours). FBI says its best translators do 100 pages a month, but because of the variety of work there are no quotas. FSTC has no quotas, nor is one mentioned for Interior.

Government recruiters look for linguistic aptitude and skills in potential language staff employees. NSA actively recruits language graduates, especially in Slavic, Middle Eastern, and Asian languages, at all levels. It offers a Cooperative Education Program, Summer Employment Program, and scholarships and looks for military language specialists who have both language and specialized experience. NSA also has an intern program, as do CRS and VOA. The Translation Division head at FSTC visits universities to recruit students who enjoy translation and have linguistic ability. He feels that knowledge of technical material can be acquired through in-house training. While the State Department does not specify a degree requirement, the work itself demands a solid educational background. Most language specialists have a BA, and advancement in rank tends to parallel higher academic degrees. Long exposure to a foreign language and culture is required of those who will translate into that language. Like State, CRS deals with complex subject matter; both translating and interpreting may involve public exposure. The Library of Congress requires a BA and a working knowledge of two languages, with the ability to translate both ways in one of them. FBIS states a language proficiency requirement of 4 in common languages or 3 (on a 1-to-5 scale) in less common ones and a degree. CIA looks for a GPA of at least 3.5, excellent English, and the ability to learn languages. Its tests cover intelligence, psychological factors, language aptitude, and knowledge of world events. NSA administers a similar battery of tests. FBI tests both oral and written English and foreign language, requiring 4 in the native language and 2+ in the other, in addition to the language test conducted by phone. The SSA test consists of a paragraph to be translated from English into a foreign language.

With its strong professional orientation, NSA continues to emphasize education beyond the hiring stage, training new employees to bring their skills up to intermediate or advanced levels in foreign languages and furnishing special courses when needed for assignments, even sending an employee away for a year of full-time study in order to train for a new language. FBI also encourages achievement of high-level language proficiency by local training or in total immersion programs at such schools as Middlebury. Other federal units, too, attempt to increase and maintain the skills needed to produce high quality work.

Retaining language personnel whose talents have developed in a manner congenial to both employee and employer is a means of maintaining quality. Those whose fascination with language leads them as far as deciding to work with it as a career tend to find sufficient variety and challenge within their chosen field, given working materials suited to their intellectual and linguistic levels. Career ladders that offer senior personnel the opportunity for advancement in rank without having to assume less satisfying administrative functions have been successful at State, NSA, FBIS, FBI, and NISC, indicating a recognition of the value of keeping language personnel in their specialty.

The number of languages encountered and the quantity of translation needing attention have resulted in a considerable amount of contract translation. Here again agencies differ in the type of contractors they engage as well as in rates of payment and means of controlling quality. JPRS, the largest employer of freelance translators, acts as broker for other agencies as well as providing CIA with translations, summaries, excerpts, abstracts. Rates start as low as $26 per 1,000 words, rising according to language, material, and ability of the contractor, who can expect rate increases as his skills become known. The State Department, which pays the highest rates among government agencies, makes use of contractors for interpreting, translating, and other services. The translation that is done outside the department is largely into foreign languages. Like JPRS, State tests its contractors and monitors performance. For reasons of security, FBI prefers to engage contractors to work at headquarters on an hourly basis. Contractors take the same tests as staff translators. NIH and Interior make use of translation companies and individual contractors. Interior reviews all of the completed translations. Because of the technical nature of the material it sends out, Interior requires agencies to have an editor with an appropriate engineering specialty. Very high standards of quality and quantity are maintained at Wright-Patterson. Contractors, who submit bids for translation jobs, are given a test passage in five languages, including Czech and Chinese. Reservists and some freelances do contract translation for NISC, which also uses translation agencies. All of the contract work at the Patent Office is given to agencies. Rates are scaled according to time and language, with rush Asian language translations at the top of the scale. All translation work at the National Aeronautics and Space Administration (NASA) is administered by a contractor whose staff of two is responsible for subcontracting the translations, which come not only from Washington headquarters but also from field centers. The quality of translation is said to be "first-draft level." Evaluation is difficult, given the volume of work and small editing staff, which is restricted by time to making spot checks, but the "rejection rate averages 15%, sometimes climbing as high as 25%" (16). One of the subcontractors has found that its machine translations are more likely to be accepted. NASA has high praise for the quality of translations it has received from Europe.

Translation excellence in the Federal Government means, minimally, an accurate transfer of information between languages; to this may be added subtlety and felicity of style. What is required for a good translation varies according to material and circumstances. A translator who works with Social Security claims needs a sharp eye and a good memory in order to identify quickly significant data from what would appear to an inexperienced person to be a bewildering assortment of documents. A State Department interpreter at an international conference needs high levels of perception and judgment as well as a literary translator's sensitivity to nuances and ironies. Achievement of excellence begins with selecting staff members who have broad backgrounds and linguistic ability and who find satisfaction in using and developing them. They are expected to have sufficient training to bring skills to a level of expertise appropriate for the work that will be encountered. Applicants for both staff positions and potential contract language specialists are tested for proficiency. Outside language assignments are monitored by editing contract translations, rejection of unacceptable work, and cancellation of contracts when translations too frequently fail to meet standards. Improvement and expansion of subject knowledge and languages through additional training and the development that occurs in an employee who finds challenge and reward in translation, together with a career ladder that encourages higher-level employees to continue in the work they prefer, have proven successful in maintaining the quality of in-house production. We are reminded from time to time of the embarrassment to the United

States caused by an interpreter's error a number of years ago. That a single error is cited repeatedly over a period of time points at once to the need for excellence in government translation and interpretation and to the fact that it is usually achieved.

REFERENCE

Crump, Ted. *Translations in the Federal Government: 1985*. Chevy Chase, MD 20815: Ted Crump, 2719 Colston Drive.

Current And Future Translation Trends In Aeronautics and Astronautics

TIMOTHY J. ROWE

Scientific areas of specific importance in translation have tended to parallel general developments in the aerospace industry. Naturally, scientific areas in which the U.S. is more advanced than other countries tend to have lower translation volumes, while areas in which foreign research is more advanced tend to generate a larger volume of translation.

Current Trends

For the most part, however, a large amount of current aerospace translations continue to pertain to basic research being conducted in the Soviet Union. The classic areas of aerospace research, including fluid dynamics, aircraft propulsion systems, airframe technology, communications, theoretical modeling and simulation, spacecraft systems, plasma physics, astronomy, and remote sensing continue to provide the bulk of material for translation from Soviet scientific literature.

Many recent translation trends in aerospace directly reflect the increase in the internationalization of the aerospace industry, as well as the recent shift from space exploration to the commercialization of space through the Space Shuttle, Spacelab, and in the future through the Space Station. This is evident in the increase in translation volume from European languages, particularly German and French, as well as Japanese and Chinese. The recent increases in cooperation among multinational government, commercial, and research organizations have resulted in increases in translation of basic scientific research, organizational communications, and reference material.

Similarly, the recent emphasis on the commercialization of space research has resulted in new financial incentives for private and government organizations to promote space research for profit. As a result, foreign aerospace companies have a substantial incentive to work together to ensure that they remain competitive in commercial ventures. Although English continues to be the working language of the international aerospace community, the increase in international cooperation has led to significant increases in translation within Europe, between Europe and the U.S., and between Europe and the third world. This trend indicates a shift in aerospace translation in the U.S. toward a diversification of the nature of material to be translated. Although basic scientific data remains the largest sector of translation material, business correspondence, proposal and contract material, handbooks and other reference materials are becoming a larger part of aerospace-related translation. This trend appears to be equally important in the U.S. and in Europe.

The trend towards the commercialization of space research has also caused a new emphasis on increasing the quality of aerospace translations. As the private sector begins to step up its reliance on scientific literature and reference works in translation, the demand for exceptionally high-quality, rapid translation of aerospace documents is increasing. Unlike many government translation projects, where quality and turnaround time may be sacrificed for a bargain-basement price, the international business community cannot afford to settle for low-quality or inaccurate translations which are delivered too late to do any good. This trend has had a secondary effect on the aerospace industry, in that many companies are becoming sophisticated consumers of translation services. Corporate scientific and technical librarians who process translations are increasingly learning more about the translation market in order to get the most for their company's translation budget. This has had positive effects on the quality of aerospace translations in the private sector. One effect is that translation services which have provided poor quality translations in the past must now either improve their quality or lose business, as their past performance is now judged by more informed consumers.

Nonetheless, there still is some resistance to translating scientific and technical material on the part of corporate resource managers who allocate funds for translation. Some managers continue to believe that if a particular foreign scientific report is truly important, it will eventually appear in translation in an English language publication anyway. Many times these managers will refuse to spend a few hundred dollars for a translation, while at the same time allocating thousands of dollars to replicate scientific data that was already available in the foreign document. Fortunately, these outmoded ideas are rapidly changing. As the fast-paced environment of the international aerospace industry requires that companies act quickly, managers are increasing their use of translated materials. They are starting to recognize that their competition is making good use of foreign material in translation also, and that money spent on translation often equates to a good return on investment. In an international context, many managers also are beginning to recognize that their European and Japanese competition has no reservations at all about having material translated, despite translation production costs which are higher in Europe and Japan than in the U.S.

The trend toward more corporate sophistication in translation also has generated a demand for secondary language services, such as the production of corporate-wide computer glossaries with a controlled vocabulary, and close cooperation with machine translation and foreign language computer typesetting services. These secondary services are particularly important for the aerospace industry, where very large multinational corporations are the main consumers of translation services. Industries which are dominated by smaller companies may not have the resources to work with extensive computer glossaries or machine translation projects.

Unfortunately, the trend towards an increase in translation quality does not necessarily hold true for the government aerospace translation projects mentioned previously. As the low bidders continue to win government contracts, one of the easiest ways that translation service can be provided at very low prices is by cutting back on editing, proofing, and quality control, thereby lowering the quality of the translation. Of course, sometimes high-quality translations are indeed provided; however, the problem is that due to the lack of editing and quality control of translations, high quality can not be guaranteed, or even expected, for the majority of government-sponsored translations.

The problem of poor quality is evident in many ways; the most glaring examples are blatant mistranslations, such as when *Luft- und Raumfahrt* ("aeronautics and astronautics") is translated as "air- and space-travel"; when *Start Termin* ("launch date") is translated as "starting time"; when *carga útil* ("payload") is translated as "useful cargo"; or when *kosmicheskiy apparat* ("spacecraft") is translated as "space apparatus." Other indicators of poor quality, again usually resulting from a lack of adequate editing and quality control, are poor English wording, inconsistent use of grammar, poor graphics reproduction, and incorrect use of scientific English terminology.

Recent increases in the sophistication of the aerospace translation consumer indicate that currently one of the most effective methods for increasing quality is to stress the editing and proofing of translations, rather than initially being overly concerned with the original translation. The reason for this is that the technical accuracy of even a mediocre translation may be significantly improved by good editing, with the result that a relatively high quality translation can be produced with a modest amount of additional effort. Most importantly, a consumer who is knowledgeable in translations may now be able to participate in the quality control process more then he has in the past. This not only gives the consumer more direct control over translation quality, it also allows the consumer to evaluate translation services more accurately.

Another factor that has had an interesting effect on the quality of aerospace-related translations is the fact that many highly qualified scientists from foreign countries have immigrated to the U.S. Many of these scientists are only able to find work as translators due to the restrictions imposed on foreigners in defense industries. Unlike other scientific areas, where foreign experts may be hard to find in the U.S., foreign-trained aerospace scientists from Europe, the Soviet Union, Japan, and other countries are often employed as translators. This trend has had both positive and negative effects on translation quality. As the foreign-trained experts are knowledgeable in aerospace terminology, often their translations are technically very accurate. However, as their knowledge of English is sometimes less than adequate, their translations into English often require substantial editing by a native English speaker. If this editing stage is neglected, poor quality translations may be produced.

In addition to quality, the trend towards increasing the availability of translations that have been done is an important factor in aerospace translation. Although the current scientific and technical information processing capabilities of the government and private industry are impressive, there is a tendency for each organization to keep its translations restricted to in-house use. The reasons for this include concerns of possible copyright questions, the fundamental lack of incentive on the part of private industry to share any information at all, the logistical problem of establishing information sharing networks, and the lack of duplication check skills of translation and library personnel. Although translation clearinghouses such as the National Technical Information Service (NTIS) and the National Translations Center of the University of Chicago library do provide information sharing and translation duplication check services, at present they are under-utilized by the private sector. They will only prosper in the future if more translation producers contribute substantial numbers of translations on a continuing basis. By increasing the capabilities of these translation clearinghouses, their status and visibility would be increased, thereby benefiting the entire aerospace information community. This, however, is a long-term goal for private industry. Currently, many large corporations do not even have effective information-sharing networks in place to make translations done by one division available to different divisions of the same company.

Important Scientific Areas in Aerospace Translation

In many cases, increases in translation of scientific material from certain countries reflect an interest in particular areas of science in which the state of scientific research in those countries is advanced. For example, a large part of the recent increase in German translation can be attributed to the advances in the area of materials science research in microgravity (weightlessness) conducted by West German scientific organizations. As part of the commercialization of the space environment, where the microgravity and vacuum of space are utilized to produce materials and metal alloys that would be impossible to produce economically under the influence of the Earth's gravity, materials science has become a very important part of space research. German science organizations have been active in this area of research since the early seventies, and have devoted a significant amount of their national resources to this area.

In fact, German scientists had been conducting extensive experiments in this area quite some time before the first important materials science experiments were conducted on board the American Skylab in the mid-seventies. This enabled the German scientific community to establish itself as one of the early leaders in this discipline and is the reason why this area of research will continue to generate a significant amount of translation for the forseeable future. The recent Spacelab mission, which was launched in November 1985 on the Space Shuttle, and which was the first Spacelab mission under the operational control of the West German Space Operations Center, contained a large number of important materials science experiments. It can be expected that a large part of the scientific reports resulting from this mission will be available initially only in translation.

Soviet research in materials processing in microgravity has also provided valuable information for U.S. researchers, as the Soviets have been able to carry out more long-exposure experiments on their Salyut-Soyuz orbital platform than have U.S. astronauts on the Shuttle. The ability to conduct long-term experiments has also allowed the Soviets to achieve significant advances in space biology and medicine. The result has been that U.S. scientists are able to obtain important information on space experiments requiring several life-cycle generations in large part only from translations of Soviet scientific literature. This trend is expected to continue at least until the nineties, when the American Space Station becomes operational.

Similarly, research in composite materials has received substantial interest from the aerospace scientific community. The use of composite materials, such as carbon fiber reinforced plastics (CFRP) and superplastic "sandwich" laminated materials, is one of the most promising methods for reducing weight and increasing the strength of aircraft structural components. Translations from German and French source material pertaining to composite materials have increased recently and are the result of many co-related factors. One factor is that Germany is considered to be a world leader in glider technology; the reason for this is that unlike the U.S., Germany has fewer ground facilities for expensive motorized private aircraft. Therefore, less expensive gliders are preferred by private pilots. The thriving German glider industry is a very important innovator in composite materials, as the industry has been quick to respond to the significant market demand for less expensive and better-performing gliders using components made of lightweight composite materials. As both Germany and France have advanced composite materials research programs, the trend toward more translations in this area from German and French source material will certainly continue for at least the next 5–10 years.

Currently, one of the most important areas of scientific importance to the aerospace industry is the development of advanced industrial ceramics. This area is also one of the most important areas for aerospace translations, as a significant amount of the basic and applied research pertaining to this area has been pioneered in Japan and in Europe. Although industrial ceramics have important, and strategic, applications in heat and corrosion resistant engine and turbine components, interest in this area has been significant only in the past few years. Since the seventies, however, industrial ceramics research has been given a very high priority by Japanese and European research teams sponsored by their respective governments. This has led to an impressive amount of information which has been available only in translations from Japanese and European source material, particularly patents and research journal reports.

In fact, the importance of translations in this area was emphasized in a recent edition of the American Ceramic Society *Bulletin*, which stated that "The U.S. has largely lost the electronic ceramics business to Japan, and is unlikely to regain it. A widening gap is seen in the evolution between the U.S. and Japan in the second major industrial category of advanced engineering ceramics." Other important advanced research efforts are currently being conducted in Germany, France, and China. Translations from these countries pertaining to industrial ceramics will certainly continue to increase in importance and volume for many years to come. Increased U.S. research efforts in this area, such as those conducted by the NASA Lewis Research Center as well as by General Motors, will only stimulate the demand for translations as they attempt to catch up with foreign advances.

In addition to ceramics, translation from Japanese scientific source material in general has increased substantially due to Japanese advances in aerospace industrial capabilities, as evidenced by their active rocket and satellite development programs. Japanese advances in areas such as electric ion engines for satellite guidance and control have provided valuable information for U.S. scientists. A large part of this information has been available only in translation. The need for an increase in Japanese translation capabilities has even moved the U.S. Congress to action; in November 1985, the Senate passed the "Japanese Technical Literature Act." This act instructs the Commerce Department to publish an annual directory of U.S. companies and professional societies that are involved in Japanese translations, as well as a list of Japanese technical documents that have been translated by federal agencies. Governmental interest in Japanese translation will surely contribute to a substantial increase in Japanese aerospace translation.

Similarly, advances in China's aerospace capabilities continue to cause an increase in the amount of translation from Chinese. One of China's most important recent accomplishments in aerospace technology was the launching of several satellites; these satellites were placed into orbit using advanced cryogenic third stage launch vehicles. Other significant achievements include the development of sophisticated spacecraft tracking capabilities, particularly in the areas of orbital dynamics and recovery systems, as well as impressive advances in celestial mechanics and astronomical modeling. These advances have resulted in a significant increase in aerospace-related translation from Chinese. Private sector aerospace translations from Chinese are also expected to increase, as more commercial joint ventures pertaining to aerospace industries are undertaken by Chinese, U.S., and European partners.

The fact that European countries are increasing their technical expertise in the commercial production and world-wide marketing efforts of advanced aircraft, components, avionics, and other aerospace-related products has meant that U.S. industry has also recently shown an increase in translation from European languages. In previous years, American aerospace companies could count on a stable foreign market for their goods and services, due to a lack of substantive competition from foreign companies. This situation has changed, requiring American companies to pay more attention to foreign aerospace developments. This should also lead to a further increase in translation from European source material.

The internationalization of the aerospace industry has fostered the development of international aerospace commercial and governmental organizations due to the tremendous costs involved with aerospace ventures. Commercial associations primarily consist of joint efforts to market specific aerospace technology. Examples of these would be the joint British-French Concorde supersonic transport, the European Airbus aircraft and the Ariane launch vehicle consortium. Intergovernmental organizations, such as the European Space Agency, are more concerned with large-scale international projects such as the European participation in the Shuttle program with the ESA-sponsored Spacelab, and the Columbus program with which the ESA will participate in the American Space Station project.

Both of these types of international aerospace organizations will continue to generate substantial amounts of world-wide translation work. The increase in the number of countries and organizations with advanced aerospace capabilities indicates that international commercial and governmental relationships will be increasingly multilateral rather than bilateral, and will be less dominated by U.S. interests. Therefore, unlike the translation trends of the past, in the future it can be assumed that increasing amounts of this translation work will be from non-English source material into non-English text. The most important language pairs will probably continue to be from and into French and German, but as these international organizations increase their participation with non-traditional trading partners, other languages such as Japanese, Chinese, Spanish, and Italian will continue to become more important.

Future Trends: Europe, Space Commercialization, and the Space Station

Future translation trends in the aerospace sciences will be shaped to a large degree by several factors interacting with one another. It is apparent that the combination of the internationalization of the aerospace industry, together with the commercialization of space through the Space Shuttle and the international cooperation in Space Station research, will act together to significantly increase the demand for translations in the aerospace sciences. Following the historical pattern, the U.S. once again is beginning to enter a significant growth period for translations pertaining to aeronautics and astronautics.

Unlike previous growth periods, however, the current impetus for increases in translation volume is based on several very different factors, rather than just one or two events or situations. This means that the current growth period will not only be more substantial than previous periods; it should also last much longer and have a greater impact on the industry as a whole. The tremendous commercial opportunities of future space ventures will require substantial international cooperation because of the enormous capital expenses involved. This indicates that extensive translation programs will play a large part in the success or failure of space ventures and international commercial aviation projects. Already, translations have become a vital factor in ensuring competitiveness in the international marketplace for aerospace goods and services. This trend certainly will continue in the future. It will become even more significant as European organizations gain expertise in multinational aerospace projects.

At this time, one of the prime vehicles for the future commercialization of space is the American Space Transportation System, consisting primarily of the Space Shuttle and the Space Station. The Shuttle already has made significant contributions to many different commercial projects, including those of foreign consumers. The potential for future increases in the demand for translations is also evident in the international make-up of the Space Station. NASA has already signed memoranda of understanding with the European Space Agency, Canada, and Japan. These agreements provide a framework for international cooperation in conducting design studies and future use requirements of the Space Station. The exact nature of the Space Station elements to be provided by the international partners were to be finalized in the spring of 1986; however, it was already assumed that the Columbus space platform of the European Space Agency would be one of the most important elements of the Space Station system. As could be expected, one of the main scientific objectives of the European Columbus program will be materials science experiments and other experiments dealing with microgravity.

In addition, other more exotic long-term areas of aerospace research will also utilize foreign developments. One example would be research on hypersonic and transatmospheric aircraft. These advanced aircraft would be able to take off from conventional airport runways, reach near-orbital speeds (about Mach 25), enter low Earth orbit and then re-enter the atmosphere to land at another airport. Aircraft such as these would be capable of flying from Los Angeles to Tokyo in a little over two hours. Avanced versions of such aircraft would provide a cheaper, more flexible alternative to the Space Shuttle for placing satellites or other experimental payloads into orbit. Realization of this type of advanced technology is dependent, among other areas, upon further research on ceramic engine components, turbomachinery, and cryogenic fuel systems technology. Developments in these areas would lead to advances in ramjet and scramjet (supersonic combustion ram-jet) engines, which would be capable of providing the thrust needed for such an "aerospace plane." It is certain that a significant portion of the basic research needed for developments in these areas would come from Japan, Europe, and the Soviet Union.

This becomes even more important when viewed in a strategic con-text. The actual impetus for the development of transatmospheric transport aircraft is not to provide quicker passenger service between the U.S. and foreign counties. Instead, transatmospheric aircraft are being seriously considered because they would provide the Air Force with an invaluable "orbit-on-demand" vehicle with which to quickly launch satellites necessary for Strategic Defense Initiative programs. Other future aerospace-related SDI research projects will require large amounts of translation in many scientific areas. These include laser and plasma physics, guidance systems, cryogenic equipment, infrared detectors, energy storage systems, mass accelerators, and optics. Primary sources of information on foreign developments in these areas will be from the Russian, German, Japanese, and Chinese scientific literature.

Other possible future projects, such as a lunar base or a joint U.S.-Soviet manned mission to Mars, would also be highly dependent upon substantial international cooperation. These projects would also re-quire large amounts of translation work in many different scientific areas.

From the projects mentioned above, it is easy to see how each fac-tor involved in future space research affects other factors. When viewed as a whole it is evident that international cooperation and the need for mutual understanding in the aerospace industry are bringing about the beginning of the greatest growth period in aerospace translation yet seen in the U.S. From a long-term perspective, recent congressional reports indicate that by the turn of the century space commerce will be a half a trillion-dollar industry. Of course, budget cuts and other unforseen events such as the loss of the Space Shuttle Challenger may make this estimate overly optimistic.

The increase in competition from foreign corporations and interna-tional consortiums will create substantial challenges for the U.S. in-dustry to meet in the future. Translation suppliers who are able to meet the demand for high quality, accurate translations will certainly benefit from these opportunities. As an integral part of the aerospace industry, these suppliers will continue to form a vital part of the competitiveness of the American aerospace industry in the future.

REFERENCES (IN ORDER OF USE)

1. Roland, A. "Model Research – A History of the NACA," NASA SP–4103, NASA, Washington, D.C., 1985.
2. Newell, H. E. "Beyond the Atmosphere – Early Years of Space Science," NASA SP–4211, NASA, Washington, D.C., 1980.
3. "NASA 1986 Long-Range Program Plan," NASA, Code LB, Washington, D.C., August 1985.
4. "NASA Space Systems Technology Model" sixth edition, Executive Summary, NASA TM–88175, NASA, Code R, Washington D.C., June 1985.
5. Wilford, J. N. "Biggest Shuttle Crew Begins First Foreign-Run Mission," *The New York Times*, October 31, 1985.
6. Sahm, P. R. "Weightless Space as a Laboratory: The Spacelab D1 Mission," ESA *Bulletin*, No. 43, August 1985, pp. 68–76.
7. Malmejac, Y. et al. "Challenges and Perspectives of Microgravity Research in Space," ESA BR-O5, October 1981, European Space Agency, Paris, France.
8. Langbein, D. "Materialforschung unter Mikrogravitation" (Materials Science in Microgravity), *Spektrum der Wissenschaft*, April 1984, pp. 28–42.
9. Regel', L. L., ed. "Salyut-6-Soyuz, Materialovedeniye i Tekhnologiya" (Salyut-6-Soyuz, Material Sciences and Technology). Moscow: "Nauka" Press, 1985.
10. Naumann, R. J. "Materials Processing in Space: Early Experiments," NASA SP–443, NASA, Washington D.C., 1980.
11. Lo, R. E. "Europaeische Raumfahrt-Transportsysteme" (European Space Transportation Systems), DGLR, (German Aerospace Society), Annual Convention, *Proceedings*, Bonn West Germany, September 9, 1985, pp. 1–24.
12. Furniss, T. "ESA Aims at 2001," *Space World*, May 1985, p. 26.
13. Robinson, C. A. "Europe's New Independence," *Aviation Week & Space Technology*, June 4, 1984, p. 11.
14. Clever, J. "Bedeutung weltweiter Kooperation" (The Importance of World-Wide Cooperation), *Aerokurier*, 28 (December 1984): 1321–1322.
15. Reichhardt, T. "Toward an International Solar System," *Space World*, April 1985, pp. 24–26.
16. Lenoe, E. M. and Meglen, J. L. "International Perspective on Ceramic Heat Engines," *American Ceramic Society Bulletin*, 64 (February 1985): 271–275.
17. "Research on the Applications of and Material Resources for Fine Ceramics," *Research Report* No. 113, Office of Science and Engineering, Institute of Natural Resources, Tokyo, Japan, December 13, 1983.
18. Large, A. J., "Pace Picks Up in Translations of Japanese Technical Articles," *The Wall Street Journal*, December 27, 1985, p. 11.
19. Ogata, M. and Mizusawa, H. "Discussion on the Progress and Future of Japanese Satellite Communication," *Mitsubishi Gunki Giho* (Mitsubishi Journal of Military Hardware), 59 (1985): 408-412.

20. O'Lone, R. G. "Japan Setting Higher Aerospace Goals," *Aviation Week & Space Technology*, November 21, 1983, pp. 16-18.

21. Tang, T. B. "The Chinese Aviation and Space Industries–An Overview," *Xian dai jun shi* (Conmilit), Hong Kong, December 1983, pp. 12-17.

23. Langereux, P. "Next Launch of the (Chinese) Long March 3 Rocket at the End of 1985 or Beginning of 1986," *Air et Cosmos*, no. 1019, October 20, 1984, pp. 80–81.

22. Lenorovitz, J. M. "China Plans Upgraded Satellite Network," *Aviation Week & Space Technology*, November 21, 1983, pp. 71- 75.

23. Reinharz, K. K. "European Aspects of Using the Space Station," ESA *Bulletin*, No. 41, February 1985, pp. 42–50.

24. Furniss, T. "Columbus: The European Role," *Space World*, April 1985, pp. 21–23.

25. Finke, W. "Die bemannte Raumfahrt in den neunziger Jahren– Eine europaeische Perspektive" (Manned Spaceflight in the Nineties–A European Perspective), presented at the International symposium "Towards Columbus and Space Station," Bonn West Germany, October 2, 1985, pp. 1–9.

26. Feazel, M. "Europe Pushes Space Station Role," *Aviation Week & Space Technology*, June 18, 1984, pp. 16–17.

27. Sax, H., "Columbus–Ein Konzept zur Zusammenarbeit Europas mit den USA im Raumstationsprogramm" (Columbus–A Concept for European Participation with the USA in the Space Station Program), DFVLR *Nachrichten*, no. 42, (June 1984): 19–25.

28. Haggerty, J. J. "The Outlook for Space Commercialization," *Space World*, May 1985, pp. 20–25.

29. Register, B. M. "Boosting Business into Space," *High Technology*, October 1985, pp. 53–54.

30. Grey, J. "The New Orient Express–The Hypersonic Transport," *Discover*, January 1986, pp. 73–81.

Translation Excellence in the Private Sector

COORDINATOR: SUE ELLEN WRIGHT; CONTRIBUTORS:

S. EDMUND BERGER, DORIS GANSER, KURT GINGOLD,

JOSEPHINE THORNTON

A Definition of Translation Excellence

Translators working in the manufacturing fields can only envy their colleagues on the engineering side when it comes to quality control. Unfortunately there is no simple mechanical or electronic way to gauge the accuracy of a translation. Skilled professionals may actually disagree on the characteristics which exemplify an acceptable translation. In many respects this inability to arrive at a single standard reflects the varying purposes for which translations are produced.

Hence the collaborators in this article have been chosen specifically because they represent different branches of the private sector. Josephine Thornton of the Mellon Bank in Pittsburgh is head of an in-house team of translators. Kurt Gingold, now an independent freelancer, was for many years the sole in-house translator for a major chemical manufacturer. Doris Ganser operates a translation bureau, and Ed Berger is an independent freelancer. Sue Ellen Wright has worked as the in-house translator for a company in the automotive field and as both a freelancer and a bureau operator.

In compiling the data for this paper, the contributors responded to a series of questions touching upon issues pertinent to excellence in translation. Even simple definitions varied from participant to participant:

> I view excellence in translation as consistent, accurate rendition, in flawless target language, of all thoughts expressed in the source language. (Berger)

> A translated document should serve the same function in the

target language that was achieved by the source language text. A utilitarian text will be utilitarian, an informational document informational, and an advertising passage should draw on the linguistic patterns of the target culture in the same way the original captures its audience. (Wright)

These definitions reflect a perception of what translation ought to be. Inherent in this view is the premise that we must translate *ideas*, not words, and that the finished text should read as if it were an original composition in the target language. In effect, the translator's control of the text should act as a membrane whose selective permeability allows free flow of concepts without permitting foreign idioms and sentence structure to penetrate the barrier. In another – self-defined as pragmatic – vein:

An excellent translation is one that is considered excellent by the client for whom it was prepared. Presumably the client will consider a translation excellent if it exactly fulfills the purpose for which he requested it. . . . Since the translator more often than not does not know what this purpose is . . . , it is frequently difficult to know what aspects of the translation he should concentrate on. (Gingold)

Although there is an element of cynicism in the above observation, it takes cognizance of the fact that translations are produced for different purposes, using different procedures.

Commercial and technical translations can be divided into essentially two categories: Not for publication and for publication.

1. Not for publication

1.1 "Quick and dirty"

This category usually includes such things as telexes, telecopy, invoices and routine correspondence. Text presentation may be anything from a handwritten notation on the original, a dot-matrix printout, or just an oral précis. The transition from this category to the next involves a gray area where even extended texts may be given a rapid oral, handwritten, or draft-print treatment.

1.2 "For information only"

Texts intended strictly for in-house applications, such as for research, or in deciding whether to quote, may be given less attention and care in text production than publication-quality translation.

Not-for-publication translations are generally commissioned with the understanding that the job will be done quickly and with minimum expenditure of time and effort. Nonetheless, it is imperative that the text be accurate. "We try to combine accuracy, speed, clarity and brevity. Unfortunately, speed sometimes must come before clarity and brevity, but accuracy is a must.... Speed without accuracy is useless." (Thornton) "As to balance between speed and accuracy, mine is usually tipped toward accuracy." (Berger) "Speed is frequently an important factor, but I would never put that ahead of completeness or accuracy." (Gingold)

As a consequence, I have always disliked the request, "Just give me a rough translation," not because I object to providing a quick summary of a text, but because the phraseology implies that the results will probably be less than accurate. (Wright)

2. For publication

2.1 "Copier-ready" copy

Many texts, such as material specifications or testing guidelines, are produced for dissemination to a company's clients or for widespread in-house use. These documents will not be typeset, but they will be typed or printed out in flawless format, with graphics prepared so that they resemble the original.

2.2 True "camera-ready" copy

These texts will serve as the original for lithographic printing. Such materials often include advertising copy, brochures, books, and other highly critical materials.

"We must use immensely greater care in these assignments. First of all, it is very important to assemble the proper translating and editing team in advance. If the original translator is not quite familiar with the subject area, the editor must be. We also need fastidious proofreaders who have not been exposed to the work before." (Ganser) The translation is read against the original to catch discrepancies, and independently to check intelligibility of the target text. Advertising copy may get special attention: "For one headline, we sometimes write 20 or more versions before one pops up that best gets the point across." (Ganser)

Setting Priorities

1. Speed

At one time or another all translators find themselves under pressure to work more rapidly than they think desirable. It can be difficult to "educate" a client in the time factors required for quality translation. Clients may spend weeks, even months, preparing a complex text and then be distressed to find that it will take the translator more than a few hours or days—or even weeks—to produce the translation.

"In my experience, clients are very difficult to educate in this matter. Furthermore, even if we could educate our clients, there are many occasions in which there is a legitimate need for rush service. . . . Other professionals have to deal with emergency situations from time to time, and so do translators. In my opinion, there [is sometimes] a little too much whining about allegedly impossible requirements. Of course, non-salaried translators have the right to expect higher payment (by both bureaus and direct clients) for work that, for any reason, requires above-normal performance." (Gringold) Most translators do require a surcharge for rush material, which is probably the best educational tool there is. If a client learns that he will get better quality at a lower price if the translator doesn't have to burn the midnight oil to complete the job, he may well coordinate his efforts more efficiently in the future.

2. Accuracy

It would seem from previous comments that excellence in translation is predicated upon accuracy. Accuracy depends on two factors: grammatical/syntactical interpretation of the source text, and technical understanding of the subject matter. Total understanding of the source language and the ability to interpret syntactical elements is the *sine qua non* for any translation assignment. Without this capability no individual should call himself a translator. Technical understanding, on the other hand, derives from an amalgam of basic knowledge and research skills.

A perennial question – comparable to "which came first, the chicken or the egg?" – ponders who makes the better translator, the scientist, technician, or lawyer who also has language skills, or the trained linguist who augments a broad educational background with intensive research into assigned subject areas.

There is no easy answer. There are good translators – and bad ones, too – whose origins lie in both areas. Since much of what translators are called upon to manipulate is state-of-the-art material, it is even a rare chemist, engineer, or medical specialist who automatically knows everything there is to know about a given subject field without checking out the latest trends and terminology. Nor do many translators always have the luxury of working only in a narrow field of specialty. Hence, all translators must be researchers to an extent, even if some do have special knowledge in certain fields.

By the same token, it has been argued that the linguist-translator will probably be more equipped to provide the syntactical accuracy cited at the beginning of this section. There is no reason to assume, however, that the scientist-engineer-whatever specialist has not acquired the same "Sprachgefühl" that qualifies the language specialist for doing the same job. It all boils down to the fact that some people are good translators, and some people aren't. Origins don't seem to matter as much in the long run as individual talent.

3. Resources

3.1 Dictionaries and monolingual references

Every serious translator must make the initial investment in the basic bilingual dictionaries pertinent to his language and subject area specialties. Dictionaries are expensive, so a library has to grow gradually, and the translator should always weigh investment against return. "Access to good institutional libraries becomes critical when the subject matter is complicated." (Berger) This factor alone may even dictate where a translator locates geographically. A translator cannot exist in an intellectual vacuum or thrive in the informational hinterland.

Dictionaries are only the most obvious tool in the translator's library, however. "I should mention that we keep an extensive reference material file (cross-referenced) including mail-order catalogs from several countries, brochures from numerous foreign manufacturers, scientific articles written in the foreign language, glossaries in every imaginable field, and we update these constantly by mailing the cards in the back of technical journals which offer free literature, keeping food package labels from supermarkets, and drug labels." (Ganser)   Witness the translator as terminological pack rat!

Standard encyclopedic subject-area references, such as technical handbooks, form the backbone of an adequate library. Smart bureau operators quiz prospective translators on their resources before considering them for employment because the degree of sophistication revealed in the library reflects the translator's own expertise.

The best source of materials may be the client himself. I always ask at the outset if he or she can provide any target-language texts that are similar in content to the text in question. Product literature and catalogs are invaluable sources of information. (Wright)

3.2 Human resources

The first thing that a novice translator learns about even the best dictionaries is that the really important terms won't be there anyway, no matter how specialized the lexicon. With luck and good research skills, the answers may be found in source-language literature. Failing that, the translator can turn to a subject-field specialist, who may or may not be his client.

"I am a great believer in using 'expert consultants', both within my company and among my translator acquaintances, wherever necessary, and *after making a sincere effort to solve the problem myself*." (Gingold) "My major reason for not bothering a direct client is that I do not wish to appear ignorant." (Berger)

Obviously, such consultations are a two-sided coin. I never bother someone about a term unless I have first exhausted every other possible source, and I make certain that any questions reveal my knowledge rather than my ignorance. (Wright)   Some agencies and bureaus discourage client/translator contact, whereas others go out of their way to establish dialogue between clients and translators, encouraging them to form a communications team.

Use of a second reader provides a further check on translation accuracy. "This will usually reduce linguistic and substantive errors and detect omissions. If the second reader has specialized knowledge or has a solid knowledge of the target language, he/she can critically improve the readability of the translation." (Berger)   The ideal translator/editor relationship can evolve – perhaps in an in-house situation – where the translator works into his/her native language or language of habitual use, then the translation is read and edited by a subject area expert with native- language proficiency in the source language. Needless to say, opportunities for this kind of interaction are infrequent, and it may be an expensive procedure in all but the most critical cases.

4. Style

Many literary translators assume out of hand that technical and commercial translators are not concerned with questions of style, and some technical translators, perhaps out of a belief that stylistic considerations are out of place in their pragmatic world, eschew discussing the matter. "Style in the target language is usually not one of my main concerns. I concentrate primarily on making the translation fully intelligible. In most cases, the original text is not all that stylish anyway." (Gingold)

Nonetheless, "the translator's style should be facile, smooth and unequivocal, particularly in technical translations." (Berger)   Technical and commercial translators are, in fact, technical writers, and their work should be concise, technically accurate, consistent, and clear, as well as correct in spelling, punctuation, and grammar. In some instances, it may also be persuasive and interesting, if the source text warrants. (Bly, 1982, 1–6) Intelligible, facile, smooth, clear, and brief – all these terms describe style. In this context, style is not some sort of ability to express oneself in an original fashion or with a great deal of metaphor, which I think is perhaps the misconception which leads serious translators to claim they are unconcerned about style.

"Style changes according to the audience." (Thornton)

Alan Duff claims,

> It would be a mistake, I think, to assume that only the literary translator is concerned with problems of style. Whatever discipline he may be working in, the translator will have to consider, for instance, what *public* the work is intended for and what degree of specialist knowledge the reader is expected to have. (1981, 7)

Consequently, one must determine, for instance, whether a text is to be used by an automotive engineer or a mechanic, and choose the vocabulary and level of language accordingly.

Machine Aids

1. Text generation

Modes of text generation are directly related to the considerations discussed earlier, i.e. not for publication and publication. Informal, not-for-publication work may stop at the handwritten, draft-quality stage, but methods for reaching the final product for copier- or camera-ready material vary. Some translators do produce their initial drafts by hand, although most find this time-consuming and physically taxing. A few years ago the state-of-the-art procedure was to dictate texts for transcription by typing or word processing. Other translators who are more keyboard oriented have been producing their own texts on correcting typewriters but are rapidly shifting to word processing.

Dictation requires a smooth working relationship between the translator and the typist, and doing one's own word processing demands an openness to accepting new technology, coupled with keyboard facility. Both dictating and keyboarding require the development of the proper mind-set for text production in this fashion. Friedrich Krollmann of the West German Bundessprachenamt noted a few years ago that his people use several different methods of text generation, depending upon personal predilection. "Contrary to popular opinion, not all Germans make good dictators." This holds true, I think, for translators of any national heritage.

The method of text production affects the speed and efficiency of the translator. Effective dictation or skillful word processing can increase a translator's output considerably. For quality of final text production, word processing is ideal because the ability to make corrections and reprint perfect "original copy" virtually guarantees an attractive final product. Regardless of generation procedures, it is imperative that the translator or the typist use fresh ribbons whenever necessary, ensure that print elements are clean, and provide decent quality paper.

2. Computer aids to translation

For purposes of brevity, we have chosen not to deal with machine translation in this article.

However, beyond the use of computers for word processing, computer aids to translation are playing an ever-increasing role in enhancing translators' speed, efficiency, and accuracy. The primary application in this area is the production of interactive glossaries. Generation of client- and subject-specific glossaries ensures consistency within a given text and throughout the work prepared for a client. Specialized lexicons also provide terminological consistency if several translators work together on the same project. Computer-generated specialized materials can also be made available to colleagues working in related fields, thus providing up-to-date information rarely available in printed form.

Computer modem transmission of completed texts directly from the translator to the client provides an additional time-saving service. Communications capability takes on an enhanced significance with regard to typesetting. In the past, it has been imperative that translators and bureaus carefully proofread foreign language texts in order to locate all the typos creatively inserted by typesetters who don't know the language in question. The ultimate solution to this problem will be the direct transmission of the finished text from the translator's computer to the printer's electronic typesetting equipment, with an interface program converting the foreign characters directly from the original text, thus eliminating a common source of error.

Translation Competency

1. Choosing a translator

Translation clients are often at a loss to evaluate a translator's expertise. Traditionally in this country translators have been trained to be something other than translators—engineers, scientists, language specialists, and so forth. Only in recent years have a few competent training programs developed around the country. Jo Thornton, who enjoys the luxury of being involved in a training and certification program in her city, only hires people who have completed this or similar programs. Other purchasers of translation services are not so fortunate to have a pool of certified translators to choose from, and indeed there are competent, experienced translators available who never had the benefit of such a program because none existed at the time they were developing their skills.

One "lowest common denominator" is ATA accreditation, but even individuals involved in that program are swift to point out that this is not the ultimate solution. "I would probably not give serious consideration to hiring anyone who could not pass an accreditation exam. However, passing the exam does not really mean all that much. I have graded many passages as 'pass', simply because they did not contain more than one major error and/or a small number of minor errors, although the translation was difficult to understand and showed a lack of imagination and elegance, both of which I would consider important qualities in a translator." (Gingold)

Perhaps the most effective way to judge an individual is to request a sample translation or to subject the applicant to a translation exam using materials related to a typical job. Some people with more money and time than most check translations by having back-translations prepared to see if the result resembles the original. I am not, however, convinced that this is all that effective. The best way to check a person's work is to have it graded by a translator of known expertise or a speaker of the target language who has subject-area knowledge.

2. "Hin- und Herübersetzung" – Translation either here or there

In this country, most translators work into their native tongues or into their "language of habitual use," which in many cases is English. Even a skilled linguist, Peter Newmark says,

> ... cannot write more than a few complex sentences in a foreign language without writing something unnatural and non-native.... He will be "caught" every time, not by his non-native grammar, which is probably "better" than an educated native's, not by his vocabulary, which may well be wider, but by his unacceptable or improbable collocations.... For the above reasons, translators rightly translate into their own language. (1981, 180)

Undoubtedly there are exceptional examples of individuals who, at a very early age, had the opportunity to learn more than one language well and who acquired part of their education in both cultures, thus enabling them to move freely in both directions. Normal humans, however, had best stick to translation into their native tongue.

To guarantee freshness and popular appeal, advertising copy in particular is best prepared in the target country when possible. This practice is not without its dangers, however. Sometimes disasters result if the client loses control over the choice of translator. Foreigners are just as prone to faulty judgment as are Americans, and, instead of hiring an "expensive" professional, texts can be handed to a secretary who "knows some English," but has little knowledge of the technical matter involved, or who is incapable of writing at a sophisticated level. Perhaps we in the Anglo-Saxon world are most aware of the pitfalls of "Hinübersetzung" (translation into the foreign language) because there is probably more of it done into English by non-natives than into any other major language. Although native speakers who have interference problems or lack the proper experience and training may be guilty of carrying over source-language practice into the target language, non-natives are far more likely to produce "translated" texts which mirror the physical structure of the original. As Duff notes,

> The translator who imposes the concepts of one language onto another is no longer moving freely from one world to another but instead creating a third world – and a *third language*. It is in this third language that actors become "theatre artists," teachers "educational-pedagogical workers," and travel agents "commercial-technical specialists." (1981, 10)

So-called "British English" is almost never written in Britain but rather somewhere on the continent. It comes cheaply because continental rates are lower than in the U.S., but you get what you pay for. Translation into English for use in the U.S. market should be done by Americans or Canadians, possibly in the U.K. "Made in Germany" may be a mark of quality on an automobile, but it is the kiss of death for an English text.

Special Services

In addition to technical and linguistic expertise, the translator may be in a position to advise clients concerning critical extra-textual matters. I frequently provide information on foreign materials standards to inexperienced clients and can usually refer them to knowledgeable experts if necessary. (Wright)   A manufacturer of copiers needs to know that a German-language test pattern must conform to DIN A-4 paper size, and novice exporters can be advised on the resources available from the International Business and Trade Administration of the U.S. Department of Commerce, as well as from state and local agencies.

Although this kind of information may be worth an extra charge, generally it is to the translator's advantage to pass it on gratis. "I often tell the translator that our job is not translating for the sake of translating but rather helping our client sell a product or service overseas. The original translation itself is just an intermediate step." (Ganser) Or the translator may be assisting a foreign company in its business ventures in this country. Needless to say, if the client's business thrives and the translator has played a role in that success, an on-going relationship between the client and the translator will probably be assured. Of course, if the translator is capable of actually providing export-marketing advice or serving as an export manager, the proper remuneration is appropriate.

Conclusions

Translators in the private sector frequently embody the communications link between the translation client and his customers, suppliers, and affiliates, or they may facilitate technology transfer. It behooves translators to see themselves in this light and to strive for the kind of product that will ensure the success of the client's endeavors. By the same token, there is much a client can do in terms of time management and terminological support that will assist the translator in achieving translation excellence. Ideally, translator/client interaction can constitute a "quality circle" that will best serve the ends of all parties involved.

REFERENCES

Bly, Robert W. and Gary Blake. *Technical Writing: Structure, Standards, and Style.* New York: McGraw-Hill Book Co. 1982.
Duff, Alan. *The Third Language: Recurrent Problems of Translation into English.* Oxford: Pergamon Press, 1981.
Newmark, Peter. *Approaches to Translation.* Oxford: Pergamon Press, 1981.

The Social Responsibility of Literary Translators Today

PETER GLASSGOLD

"Languages at Work," the theme of the Association conference in 1985, raised some basic ideas about the nature of literary translation, about the situation of literary translators in America today, and about the social roles we translators are called upon to play in an age of semi-literacy.

As translators, we are concerned principally with the "how's," not the "why's," of language. *How* to turn a particular configuration of words in an alien tongue—with all its associations of time, place, and tradition; with all its semantic resonances and grammatical peculiarities—into an effective, meaningful configuration of words in our own American speech, with all *its* own associations and resonances and peculiarities.

This is very practical work, requiring both expedient judgment and finesse. A writer of an original text—call him X.—must endure the mockery of the blank page that fills, all too slowly, with words of his own style and choosing. We must re-create those words, that style of X. today—and tomorrow do the same with Y., who writes in a completely different manner. That is to say, unless we are devoted to a single author with a fairly consistent style, we have to be, in a sense, more versatile writers in our own language than the people whose writings we translate are in theirs.

As literary translators, we are specialized writers, but writers we are nevertheless. And as such, our situation in this country is essentially no different from that of other writers in the literary field: not so very good, but good enough to make us want to stay there. But in one way we are different from our fellow writers: we can even less afford to forget ourselves and feel snobbish about our work, to glory in our linguistic ability and build a scale of false social values upon it. Intrinsic to the act of literary translation is the responsibility to share special knowledge. In America today, we have a community of translators such as we have never had before—a kind of "everywhere community," to use Daniel Boorstin's descriptive phrase—whose purpose, in these decades of declining standards of literacy, is both renovative and innovative.

Before I expand on this dual role of renovation and innovation, I would like to take a closer look at the present situation of the American language and the semi-literacy I have referred to, placing them in a historical and in some ways personal context.

The dynamics of American speech, at least until recently, derive from the fortuitous balance between linguistic leveling and exuberant invention—both aspects of this nation's essential pragmatism. The leveling of English provincial dialects in the North American colonies was afterward reinforced by public education and standardized spelling, as well as a profusion of newspapers and popular writing. Though not a literary country, we became a literate one. In the nineteenth century, the ease with which Americans invented words to fit their new circumstances was astonishing to foreign visitors. And please note: this was not inventiveness limited by class. Further, as new words became accepted, they were properly spelled, were subject to normative grammatical usage, and were pronounced more or less in the same manner countrywide.

American speech together with American schooling, by democratizing literacy, laid fast hold of the immigrants drawn here by the millions, allowing them, forcefully but quietly, to turn their backs on the "Old Country" (whichever one that might be) forever.

Every American has what I call a "language history" and a "language biography"—both of which impinge upon us as translators every moment of our professional lives.

"Language history" is our personal legacy. However sophisticated the language of an immigrant family may be, by the second generation it is generally reduced to "kitchen"—"kitchen" Italian, "kitchen" German, "kitchen" what-have-you. By the third or fourth generation, what typically remains are a few terms of endearment or dislike, a swear word or two, and the names of some special kinds of food. After that, the immigrant language is lost to the family—as perhaps the family is lost to itself—though it may be temporarily revived by a solitary student through initial sentimentality followed by hard work.

A "language biography" describes the way Americans acquire speech, engage their peculiar "language history" and, in the worst instances, perceive a threat in foreign languages generally. What our forebears abandoned, why seek to recover?

As translators, we do know why. We know that American society, for all its xenophobic tendencies, is essentially cosmopolitan and interdependent with the rest of the world. We know that this interdependency runs counter to bluff posturing and not so bluff gunslinging and economic exploitation—that as time goes on and America's long postwar domination wanes, a conscious openness to fresh influences is especially called for. And where the articulation and sharing of ideas is concerned, we know that translation is culture's driving wedge: today's "global village" is a spectacular dumbshow without it.

America, however, is history-blind. Our American speech has acted as a shield against the supposed menace of the "Old Country" and, as a result, against historical realities as well. American literacy developed without historical perspective, to meet contemporary needs. But in the shallowness of late twentieth-century contemporary life, packaged needs seem to require less and less a proficiency in the written word. And history-blind, we do not understand that an illiterate society is a failing society—and that American speech and American literacy are a twin inheritance.

A conservative estimate places the number of illiterate adult Americans at twenty-five million. The real figure, according to Jonathan Kozol, is more than twice that: some sixty million. There are approximately fifty thousand new book titles published in this country in a single year. Clearly, most of them go unread. Three percent of these new titles, some fifteen hundred, are translated works. And on these decidedly downbeat statistics, I will return to my discussion of the community of translators in America today and its dual role of responsibility in these sad times.

I cannot tell you precisely how many literary translators there are in America in 1985, but I can say that most of them receive honest recompense as well as public credit for their work. A translator's rights to a formal contract and a continuing share in the income from a published work are generally acknowledged. A little more than twenty-five years ago, there were in this country: no professional translators' associations, no major literary prizes for translation, no translation workshops or programs of any kind in our schools. All this has changed.

Literary translation is no longer "hidden" writing, professionally speaking.

But for all that, what are fifteen hundred new translated books a year in the face of sixty million functional illiterates and a general indifference to the printed word? Without meaning to sound foolishly grandiose or hopeful, I can say that the quality of these books counts for a great deal indeed and gives them their catalytic potential. They are, on the whole, among the better written books published in our language; they are drawn from the better writings from abroad; and among them are found proportionately more works whose influence is likely to be long range.

Again, without making extravagant claims for the curative powers of our profession in an epidemic of illiteracy, I can say that the renovative role of literary translation was recognized very early in the development of our language — and I refer now to English, not simply our own American form of it.

In the late ninth century, as a result of the Viking invasions of the east coast of England, the whole of Anglo-Saxon society came close to collapse. Alfred of Wessex, a warrior king, a skillful organizer, and a clever negotiator, was also a translator. In the last twelve years of his life, with the Scandinavian threat more or less under control, he set out to restore health to his country by literary means. In a remarkable open letter to Wærferth, bishop of Worcester, he made these observations on the state of literacy in England:

> . . . So utterly has knowledge fallen away in England that when I began to rule there were very few men on this side of the Humber who could understand their [Latin] Mass-books and Offices in English, or even translate a letter from Latin into English; and, I think, not many beyond the Humber. So few there were that I cannot even call to mind a single one south of the Thames. . . .
>
> On all this I thought, and I thought also how, before all was destroyed and burned, I saw the churches throughout England standing full of treasures and books. We had a great multitude of servants of God; but very few of them knew what was in their books, because the books were not written in their own native speech. . . .
>
> Then I bethought me how the Law was first found in the Hebrew language, and how afterwards, when the Greeks learned it, they turned it all into their own tongue, and all other books,

as well. And so, too, the Romans. . . . Therefore it seems better to me, if you all also think it, that we, too, turn some books, those which all men need most to know, into that language which we all can understand.

Alfred himself learned Latin and made translations into his Wessex English from the works of several medieval Latin writers: Saint Gregory the Great, Bede, Boethius, Orosius, and Saint Augustine. "Sometimes," he said, "I translated word for word, sometimes for sense. . . ."[1] No doubt baffled, he fell back on paraphrase or "improved" the orginal text with his own interpolations. On occasion, too, he attempted slavishly literal renderings, trying in vain to mirror Latin syntax and declensions in his own Germanic dialect.

Alfred was, in short, the first conspicuous English literary translator, learning his craft by the familiar path of painstaking trial and error. Through his patronage, and by his personal example, he turned his Anglo-Saxon realm into the most literate barbarian kingdom of the time. As he had hoped, "all the young men of England who are of free birth and have sufficient means" did in fact learn to read. His policy of education and translation was continued under his descendants until the Norman invasion. The surviving works in Old English — not an insubstantial body, especially if one includes the many translations — owe their existence to him.

The vigor of writing in English ever since Alfred is due in large measure to a steady nourishment from foreign sources. The Norman invasion, far from destroying the English language, itself brought French to the soil of England, establishing an immensely fruitful and permanent literary and linguistic bond. As Paul Auster writes in his introduction to *The Random House Book of Twentieth-Century French Poetry,*

> . . . It is not simply that French must be considered an "influence" on the development of English language and literature; French is part of English, and an irreducible element of its genetic make-up. Early English is replete with evidence of this symbiosis, and it would not be difficult to compile a lengthy catalogue of borrowings, homages, and thefts. (1982, xvii)

Auster goes on to cite the translations and "stolen" works of Caxton, Malory, and others, bringing his pantheon of translators down to the Modernists of our own day who, in the words of Ezra Pound, "make it new" — that is, they renovate.

And renovation, as I have said, is one of the two roles literary translators must play now, in a determinedly self-conscious manner. It is a conserving, not a conservative role, and it aims to introduce the saving grace of historical resonance into American speech.

In literary translation, renovation and innovation are conjoined. It is no mere coincidence that the initial thrust of American Modernism had the weight of history behind it: Pound's Provence, his medieval Paris and Italy—his China and Japan! It was the Modernists who opened our ears to the East.

We can look far beyond Modernism, however, for examples of conserving innovation that ultimately changed the face of the world. It was, after all, a verse translation of the *Odyssey* into Latin, made in the third century B.C. by the Greek slave Livius Andronicus for his master's children, that marked the beginning of a cultural revolution in the ancient Roman world. The Latin language itself, enriched by Greek—in much the same way that French came to nourish English—became the primary instrument of change in Western Europe.

At that same period, no one could have predicted the long-term effects of rendering the sacred books of the Jews from Hebrew—clearly a "dying" language—into Hellenistic Greek, the popular speech of the eastern Mediterranean.

History resonates in the language of Modernism. Without the *Odyssey*, without the classical, medieval, and Hebraic echoes and imitations, without King Alfred's legacy, could James Joyce have conceived of his *Ulysses*? Listen to these words from "The Oxen of the Sun," the episode in which human birth and childhood telescope the birth and development of English:

> In ward wary the watcher hearing come that man mildhearted eft rising with swire ywimpled to him her gate wide undid. Lo, levin leaping lightens in eyeblink Ireland's westward welkin!

And again:

> And whiles they spake the door of the castle was opened and there nighed them a mickle noise as of many that sat there at meat. And there came against the place as they stood a young learning knight yclept Dixon.[2]

In literary translation, we are well aware of the insidious lure of archaism, to give high tone to low expression in a source text, to find a word at some stratum, at *any* stratum, of the target language to fit an impossible construction. But to my mind, where the purpose is both innovative and renovative, translators may well call upon the full historical resources of their language. Recall the stylistic versatility essential to literary translation, think again of *Ulysses*, and then consider this: a "Joycean" translation of the Bible.

The Hebrew Bible is not a single book. It is a national library gathered after the dissolution of the original Jewish state, drawn from the writings of a millennium. Each book of the Old Testament has a distinctive style, ranging as it were from Piers Plowman and the "Pearl" poet to Faulkner and Hemingway. The author of Job, with his full hoard of words, is the Shakespeare of classical Hebrew. Every one of the prophets worked within an accepted and received prophetic style—there were schools of prophets—but each is recognizably different from all the others. Isaiah's exaltations and Jeremiah's denunciations, the latter so infused with sexual energy, bring to mind Milton and Blake. Ezekiel records his visions with all the doggedness of a Robinson Crusoe drawing up his accounts.

Some of the writing is just plain bad. Befuddled Chronicles stands in contrast to the elegant clarity of Samuel and Kings—as Dreiser, perhaps, to Hemingway. The later psalms tend to be overwrought imitations of earlier Davidic models, with their controlled emotionalism, and of the dignified liturgy of the First Temple. Think of the hymns of a Cranmer as compared to Country Western rhyming pieties.

English versions of the Old Testament, no matter how beautiful, have been stylistically homogenous from the first. The blameworthy prototype, I would say, is that Hellentistic Greek translation I have already mentioned, the Septuagint, made according to legend in seventy-two days by seventy-two Jewish scholars, without a single disagreement! for the then reigning Ptolemy. What a shame, when you consider the innovative/renovative possibilities available even then: the early Greek lyric poets would switch dialects in mid-poem to suit a change in musical mode, from Dorian to Aeolian to Ionian, and so on. The Septuagint became the translation model for the Latin texts that became in turn the common Biblical sources in the Christian West.

I do not mean to imply by this that the as yet untranslated "*Ulysses* Bible" will surely set America reading again. But it does open interesting possibilities of introducing history into the shape of American speech, by renovating our most widely studied text in a loving, lively, and innovative manner.

I mentioned earlier that in the United States today there is an unprecedented community of translators. Since our essential work is accomplished in solitude, our association is necessarily loose. But this allows us a flexibility that a close-ranked organization cannot have— besides, I cannot conceive of even two translators being in complete agreement on anything, let alone seventy-two! The Translation Committee of PEN American Center is based in New York, still the hub of literary activity and commercial publishing in the United States. The American Translators Association and the American Literary Translators Association, with their memberships in communications and academe, radiate across the country. Translation centers—at Columbia, SUNY-Binghamton, the University of Texas at Dallas— serve as our oases. I can think of three areas where this professional network can be most effective.

The first is pedagogical. There are now some three hundred translation programs at the university level. A pool of potential professional translators is forming—I have met students who actually intend to become translators, not novelists or poets! This trend ought to be encouraged. Ranking high among the renovative faculties of literary translation is the natural discipline it imparts to young writers.

At PEN a few years ago, we established the Renato Poggioli Award, a yearly fellowship for an unpublished translator from the Italian. I would say the Poggioli Award has proved to be the most satisfying of our annual translation prizes. Its recipients have all used their prize money to improve their Italian and further their skills as translators. All have continued and, in most cases, seen their works in progress in print. And all, without exception, are seeing their later translation work published. The establishment of Poggioli-type awards can do more good in the long run for languages of lesser currency than the proliferation of annual prizes for the "best" published translations from, say, the Macedonian or the Swiss Romansh. I would urge us all to press for practical translation studies in our schools and, wherever possible, programs of awards and fellowships to further the training of translators here and abroad.

I will turn now from pedagogy to the problem of research. As we know, there is no comprehensive, up-to-date index of published translations and translations in progress in this country—though it is my understanding that such an entity does exist in the Soviet Union, for works into Russian. The scholarly value of a translation clearing house is indisputable, and it would serve as well as a strong foil against unauthorized translations. As some of you know, the PEN Translation Committee and the American Literary Translators Association have together been working toward the establishment of a translation clearing house at the Library of Congress. But I must admit that, at the moment, the prospects are not the brightest, and it is wise for us to begin to consider alternatives. What comes first to mind is a nationwide network of research facilities, at university-based libraries and translation centers, linked by computer. A single librarian with a knowledge of translation matters and some organizing talent might conceivably pull the whole thing together within a year or, at the very least, join in PEN and ALTA's efforts to sway the Library of Congress.

The third area in which literary translators can co-ordinate effectively is in setting international legal and ethical standards for translation. In 1985, PEN American Center published *A Handbook for Literary Translators*, which contains an updated version of "A Translator's Model Contract" as well as the position paper on ethics, "The Responsibilities of Translation." The *Handbook* also includes the very first document published by the PEN Translation Committee, the "Manifesto on Translation," issued prior to its Conference on Literary Translation in 1970. Now, for the 48th International PEN Congress, held in New York in January, 1986, the Translation Committee prepared guidelines based on the essential points set forth in the *Handbook*. Should these principles be accepted, they might be enforced by PEN centers worldwide. I would hope, too, that this statement on international standards might be subsequently considered and endorsed by other literary and translation organizations, and so help bring to an end the still foreboding exploitation of translators and the unchecked existence of pirated translations.

In these pages, I have touched upon a great many matters concerning the responsibilities of literary translators, but I have said nothing whatever of the aesthetics that underlies our work—an urge to beauty grounded in poignant impossibility. What we think we long for lies tantalizingly just beyond our grasp: the perfect metaphrase of sound and sense. We imagine a total system called Language, as it were, a unified field of human communication, but know it does not and never could exist, unless we conceive too of a poetry written in mathematics.

The dream of a universal tongue will surely remain unrealized in our lifetimes, and most of us, I think, would not care to live in Babel. It is our pleasure to tramp the border marches of words, crossing back and forth between the boundaries, and carrying news that we hope will be believed and that will stay forever news.

NOTES

1. The translation by Eleanor Shipley Duckett is from her *Alfred the Great: the King and His England* (Chicago: University of Chicago Press, 1956), pp. 145–147.
2. *Ulysses* (New York: Vintage Books, 1961), pp. 385–386.

REFERENCES

Auster, Paul, ed. *The Random House Book of Twentieth-Century French Poetry*. New York: Random House, 1982.

Duckett, Eleanor Shipley. *Alfred the Great: the King and His England*. Chicago: University of Chicago Press, 1956.

Joyce, James. *Ulysses*. New York: Vintage Books, 1961.

PEN American Center. *A Handbook for Literary Translators*. New York: PEN American Center, 1985.

Anthony Kerrigan:
The Attainment of Excellence
in Translation

MICHAEL SCOTT DOYLE

Borges, Neruda, Unamuno, Baroja, Ortega. Through the translations of Anthony Kerrigan, winner of the National Book Award in 1975, the reader of English is immediately in excellent company, the best pages of Hispanic literary giants in this century.[1] Kerrigan's career as a translator has been more than an exemplary pursuit of excellence: he has attained it, and he is recognized for having done so.[2] Although there are certain intangibles regarding Kerrigan's sustained achievement—the innate, the God-given, the mysterious—, there are, on the other hand, elements for success which he himself identifies.[3]

For Kerrigan, excellence in translation is first and foremost "a question of Literature. Part of the work of a translator is in selecting good books. His first job is to find a good book to translate. You must select great literature in the other language. It begins with choosing the writer." The text in the source language must be deserving of the translator's faith. Kerrigan's weaker translations (as he sees it) have been those where the original has not merited his faithfulness: "There's no use in being faithful to something you have no faith in, nor should have any faith in." He acknowledges that "what I think I've done badly is not good stuff in the original. Bad originals don't lead to good translations." Kerrigan cannot conceive of how "you can be a great translator of a dumb book." He recalls when he was on the jury for the National Book Award: "We had a hundred books to choose from, and I simply couldn't separate content to the point where I could say, 'This translator has done such a wonderful job, the only trouble is that he's done a grand job on a dumb book'."[4] In the final instance, "Great translators have to try their hand and show their ability with important books, those that belong to the permanent repertory of world literature." And it would appear that translators have generally exercised good judgment in this regard: "Most translators are not creating garbage because they're translating things that are good. It's funny how, in a certain sense, translated literature is a better literature because it's the best from many countries."[5]

To achieve excellence in translation, one must be able "to write good English naturally. A translator is a man who can write in his own language. He should be basically a writer." This means that "a great knowledge of your own language" is required. Mastery of the target language supersedes a "knowledge of the other language, which is really secondary." For Kerrigan, this knowledge encompasses "the richness of English, the English tradition, the English language coming down from the Elizabethans, or even if you want, to go back to Chaucer." He is interested here in "the whole history of the English language and of people reading in the English language, the tradition which is bigger than any of us." He operates completely within the realm of linguistic and literary legacy: "I'm trying to represent the best possible for the English language. What I'm trying to do is to carry on the tradition of the language of Shakespeare." The translator striving for excellence is obliged to be well versed in what his own language has accomplished for generations of readers.

Once a worthy choice of author and text has been made, and the translator acknowledges that he will be striving to match the best offered by the English tradition (in an attempt to contribute to it), excellence is pursued by "measuring and pondering every word" in praxis. Kerrigan has been widely acclaimed for his success in this endeavor: "A lot of people have said good things about me there, people like Dahlberg pointing out that I never used anything but the best language at all times, the richest possible selection of words. I've never fallen into cheapness, into effects." For him, hypothetically, "the reading public is not debased, it is enlightened, and they want the very best in the language they're reading. If they can't read in Spanish, then they're reading my English, and therefore I give them the best possible English." An ideal readership appears to contribute to the translator's effort: high standards by the reading public demand to be met, and the translator must work toward this satisfaction (although, in the end, the ideal reader may be no more than a projection of the translator's own high standards and literary conscientiousness). To achieve this gratification of the reader, the translator relies heavily, necessarily, on "all kinds of reference books" and "many dictionaries."[6]

Not only must equivalences be matched from language to language, but this should be undertaken with an etymological awareness: "If you know a word has a certain etymological meaning, then you can use that word with much more discretion, intelligence, and appropriateness. Some words you have no right to use apart from their etymology. If you reduce a word to its etymology, you can never be wrong." Again, the tradition of language is brought to bear on the translator with a certain sense of obligation, duty, integrity. An appreciation of etymology leads Kerrigan to feel that: "If I can use a word correctly, with rich root meanings and so on, then it's like a little magic counter, like a keystone arch in a building."

Kerrigan also agrees that it would behoove translators to be familiar with yet another aspect of literary tradition: that of the genre or discourse in which they are working, particularly so for poetry and philosophy. That he is a poet in his own right has helped him in his translation of poetry. At the very least, a translator endowed with poetic sensibility would be far better equipped to achieve a successful translation of poetry. It is like a musician interpreting a great composer: one needs a good ear and a fine sense of melody and rhythm. For a good translation of philosophy, "You should know how to paraphrase German philosophy when it appears in another guise, such as in Spanish." Knowledge of the philosophical tradition—of its discourse—is a prerequisite in this instance. The novel, on the other hand, Kerrigan views as "an open form, all-encompassing, it's all of life. I think anybody with a general sensibility could translate a novel."

Nor is Kerrigan at all convinced that knowing the author (the possibility of the consultative venture) will help to yield a better translation. He feels that it probably should, but that this is never a given. First of all, "To ask a poet, 'What do you mean here in this line?' is not a good question. A poet is no longer the owner of that line of verse, it belongs to the reader then, and to the world." Further, there are always cases of linguistic and semantic opacity where the source language may be beyond the equivalent reach of the target language. In translating *El Central* by Cuban poet Reinaldo Arenas, Kerrigan says that he "started to consult Arenas," but the effort was futile: "I asked him about Cuban words mainly based on sugar mill operations.

But you find that there is no equivalent in English. How are you going to talk about a certain implement in a sugar mill when there is no American or English word for it, where there are no sugar mills of that type any place but Cuba?" The answer lies in improvisation and paraphrase, the translator extemporizing creatively on his faithfulness to the original. For this to succeed, knowledge again is the key: "You have got to know how it works, and be approximate in your description of that implement."[7]

With this it is evident that literalness in translation is a relative objective for Kerrigan: "I can't see any real reason to be 'al pie de la letra', verbatim, with things." Poetry especially can be jeopardized by a literal approach. With poetry "a good translator is really a writer," another poet working in English. And if the translator "thinks of himself as simply trying to get a literal exactness, he's going to give a kind of truncated version. How are you going to translate literally, word for word, a poem? Then you destroy it utterly." The translator must resort to creative paraphrase when dealing with poetry, "which is the only thing you can do" if it is to be successful. Yet in translating Borges and Unamuno, Kerrigan strove for literalness. He felt that with Borges there was "no particular reason to improvise or change" because of his natural and transparent style: "With him almost everything comes through just as he wrote it." Unamuno required a literal approach for a different reason: "It was a thought process, and you can't fool around with sequence if you're tracing thought. You have to get it pretty exact, and you can't paraphrase it too well." Each author and text will call for a different level of translation adherence to the original, and the genres and discourses themselves will dictate the degree of literal variation.

Translation workshops and theory can contribute to excellence in an indirect manner. Since the literary translator is, in the final analysis, a writer also, Kerrigan does not conceive "how you can train a man to be a professional translator any more than in creative writing courses you can train anybody to write who isn't scheduled by destiny to write." But workshops can help to make "a lot of people more literate and increase their sensibilities." Their value lies in the fact that they are "a good intellectual stimulus," though not necessarily to write. The participant in a workshop *is* learning more about his own language and "what you can use in order to bring over from the other language something into English." And the student of translation *does* practice his writing in the workshop. But of greater importance for Kerrigan is the training one receives in reading: "They will be readers, and readers are just as important. *Poetry Magazine* had a quote from Whitman: 'To have great poets, you must have great audiences'. So I think you're teaching people to read better and to read with some critical faculty." The workshop makes its greatest contribution in the sense that it will raise the level of appreciation and expectancy of readers, thus enriching the tradition of excellence in English literature by enhancing the public demand for superior quality of language in print. The original author and the translator represent a push in this direction, but the reader should constitute a challenging pull to complement their effort. Theory in the workshop functions largely in the same manner: it heightens awareness and appreciation — linguistic, semantic, and philosophical — of various aspects of translation. But neither the workshop nor the theory a translator make. They can help to hone the skills of a practitioner, but they are no substitute for practice itself or for talent — innate, God-given, mysterious — whereby one is "scheduled by destiny to write." The ability to excel in translation transcends simple know-how, and, like all gifts, it requires constant, hard work for its realization.

The attainment of excellence in tradition is aided by "publishers of good will: men of good faith who are actually interested in writers and translators, and who try to be fair." Such publishers appreciate great literature and the desire to bring it into English. They will negotiate fair contracts with the translator,[8] and the element of trust figures prominently: "If you have a good man, and you know he's doing good work and he means well by the project, then leave him alone." Kerrigan takes into account that "the essence of being anything in writing, whether you're a translator or a creative writer, is that you really are isolated, just you and your typewriter." He is concerned about "bringing in too many people on a project," where "every translator is going to translate differently, and if you ask another translator to check on a first translator's approach and the results of his work, then the second translator is going to find everything wrong because that's not the way he would have done it."

Thus the quality of a translation is best judged by "a reader of books," not another translator: "It's bad in general to ask another translator to review a translator's work. That's a blunder because the other translator is going to find it bad. If you want a bad report, you give it to another translator to look at." The translator himself, Kerrigan says, also participates with validity in judging the quality of his own work: "one has a conscience as a person and as a worker in words, a literary worker, and you have to have developed a sixth sense regarding excellence. You have to judge yourself by high standards, and it has to do with how you've judged the author's original." This sixth sense evolves from recognition and appreciation, which are then transformed into emulation:

> If it's something wonderfully written, and you have a feel for it, and you know what it can do, you keep as high a level as you possibly can in English. You don't use cheap words, especially if the author hasn't. You keep the language in the context in which it's given in the original. Then in translating you're faithful to his text, but you're also faithful to the language you're writing in, to your own language. You have a feeling for what the original author achieved, and you want to match that in English.

Whether or not felicitous emulation of the original has been achieved then falls to the verdict of an impartial, knowledgeable, and demanding reader of Literature.

Ultimately, Anthony Kerrigan strives for "not only clarity in the English language, but a certain elegance." In translating he attempts to provide "the overall picture of the man, the overall tone, as it were, and the style." His goal is to use "the best possible English to match the best possible language of the original." In doing so, he views himself as "a literary executor of the estate of the writer. I'm trying to achieve in English what the author wanted to do." Clear, elegant, and faithful ("You never want to traduce a man who has written A and call it B"), knowledgeable, flexible, and dedicated, Kerrigan works toward an "English as naked as it is glorious, and the more naked it is, the more glorious." As he concludes: "There's only so much time in the world and so much print that people can read, we might as well be reading the best possible."

Notes

1. Kerrigan received the National Book Award for the "most distinguished book of translation," *The Agony of Christianity* (Princeton, New Jersey: Princeton University Press, 1974). He has also translated works by Angel González, Francisco Brines, José Manuel Caballero Bonald, Antonio Colinas, Jaime Gil de Biedma, José Emilio Pacheco, and H. Padilla, among others. He is currently working on a new translation of Fernando Arrabal's award-winning novel (Premio Eugenio Nadal, 1982) *La torre herida por el rayo*, together with ongoing projects such as Ortega and Borges.

2. In June of 1975 Michael Smith, writing for *The Irish Times* (Dublin), called Kerrigan "a translator of genius (. . .)perhaps the greatest translator of Spanish into English."

3. The content of what follows is drawn from interviews and conversations I have had with Kerrigan over the past three years.

4. The outcome of that National Book Award was that it was given to "two women whom I had never heard of and haven't heard of since, but they did a fantastically important book, and they put it into certainly acceptable English. I don't know whether that was the best translation of the year or not, but it was the best book, and by force of insistence I got the prize that year for (. . .) the complete volumes of Mandelstam."

5. In this regard, Kerrigan adds the following: "Junk may sell where it's spouted out, but it doesn't get into world translation. Of course, there are exceptions. Stalin's mouthings and ridiculous nonsense must be in fifty or a hundred languages. But of course, those were *paid* translators, state translators, or crazy people from other countries who will translate nonsense no matter what it is. But that's not literature, it's propaganda for political purposes."

6. Kerrigan laments the fact that for him "there's no Spanish to English dictionary that's really first-rate, like Harrap's in French-English."

7. *El Central* (New York: Avon Books, 1984). Kerrigan says of this translation that it was a prose epic "I simply re-wrote. This is the first time I've ever done this. Now, Arenas knows this, and he's said, 'My God, it's better!' Well, of course, it isn't, but it's what I did. And not only is the agent delighted, and Arenas the author delighted, but the publisher who had rejected the Spanish took the English. It's not that I've made a good book out of a bad one, it's not that at all. The point is it's worked, and with the author's permission."

8. The translator's contract which he would like to see widely accepted is that which has been drawn up by the American Literary Translator's Association.

Contributors

S. Edmund Berger is a chemist and freelance translator based in Tonawanda, New York.

Richard Brod, director of Special Projects, Modern Language Association (New York City) is secretary of the Joint National Committee for Languages.

Françoise Cestac is director of the Translation Division at the United Nations (New York City).

James R. Child directs the Language Proficiency Testing Program for the Department of Defense in Linthicum, Maryland.

Ted Crump heads the Translation unit of the National Institutes of Health Library in Bethesda, Maryland.

Michael Scott Doyle, assistant professor of Spanish, University of New Orleans, is the authorized translator of Ana María Matute.

Doris Ganser heads her own translation bureau Transimpex in Kansas City, Missouri.

Peter Glassgold is editor-in-chief of New Directions and chair of the PEN Translation Committee.

Kurt Gingold has his own translation bureau, Greenwich Accredited Translations, in Greenwich, Connecticut after many years as an information specialist in private industry.

Martha Herzog is an education specialist in the Testing/Standards Division of the Defense Language Institute Foreign Language Center in Monterey, California.

Anthony Kerrigan, translator of more than forty books, is concurrently visiting faculty fellow in the Department of Sociology, senior guest scholar in the Kellogg Institute for International Studies, and translator-in-residence at the Center for the Study of Man in Contemporary Society, all at the University of Notre Dame (Indiana).

Peter W. Krawutschke, associate professor of German and Linguistics, Western Michigan University (Kalamazoo) is founding director of the Translation Center there.

Jerry W. Larson directs the Foreign Language Testing Programs and the Humanities Learning Resource Center at Brigham Young University in Provo, Utah.

Mildred L. Larson is international translation coordinator for the Summer Institute of Linguistics (Dallas, Texas) and author of *Meaning-Based Translation*.

Anna Lilova is president of the Fédération Internationale des Traducteurs. She makes her home in Sofia, Bulgaria.

Pardee Lowe, Jr. is chief of testing at the CIA Language School in Washington, D.C.

Eric Norman McMillan is translator/reviser for the World Bank in Washington, D.C.

Gabriela Mahn is testing coordinator for the SUNY-Binghamton component of the National Resource Center for Translation and Interpretation.

Patricia E. Newman, ATA President, is a technical translator and Russian instructor for Sandia National Laboratories in Albuquerque, New Mexico.

Alice Otis is associate editor for the Translation Research and Instruction Program, SUNY-Binghamton.

György Radó has been editor-in-chief of *Babel*, FIT journal, since 1975. He lives in Budapest, Hungary.

Marilyn Gaddis Rose is founding director of the Translation Research and Instruction Program, SUNY-Binghamton.

Timothy Rowe is translation coordinator at the NASA Scientific and Technical Information Facility in Linthicum Heights, Maryland.

Michele J. Stern has just received her MA in Social Sciences (translation) from the University Center at Binghamton (SUNY).

Ben Teague, a scientific/technical translator in Athens, Georgia and past ATA president, chairs the ATA Accreditation and Publications Committees.

Josephine Thornton heads the translation section at the Mellon Bank in Pittsburgh and teaches translation at the University of Pittsburgh.

Sue Ellen Wright is co-founder of Linguistic Information Specialists, Inc. in Berea, Ohio after several years of in-house translating and university teaching.

Call for Proposals:
Technology as Translation Strategy

MURIEL VASCONCELLOS, GUEST EDITOR

Work is now underway on the volume "Technology as Translation Strategy," volume II of the American Translators Association *Series*. It is planned to cover the following topics.

I. The translator and... WORD PROCESSING

    A. Hardware: ergonomics, display and printing of foreign languages, recent breakthroughs, ideas on the drawing-board
    B. Software: latest developments, features of special interest to translators, word counts, future directions
    C. Translator strategies for getting the most out of WP
    D. Networking between systems: to clients, to translation agencies, to MT service bureaus
    E. The ideal translator workstation

II. The translator and...the LEXICAL DATA BASE

    A. The major databases: latest news, availability to translators, availability to users in the U.S.
    B. New developments originating in the U.S.
    C. System networks, access to LDBs in multitasking environments
    D. The personal LDB
    E. Translator strategies for getting the most out of LDBs

III. The translator and...MACHINE TRANSLATION

    A. Overall perspective, recent developments and trends
    B. Interactive MT
    C. Pre-editing: pros and cons, review of natural text, customized input languages, automated technology

D. Translator strategies for getting the most out of MT: postediting, participation in dictionary-building, management of the working environment

E. MT for the independent translator, in a multivalent translation agency, in a service bureau limited to MT

F. Approaches to the evaluation of MT

G. Criteria for selecting an MT system: the independent translator, the large installation

H. Expected trends

Members are urged to participate at this time by submitting to the guest editor a list of *two or three* topics they would be most interested in contributing to, together with a one-sentence summary for each of these topics emphasizing the approach they would plan to adopt. The deadline for receipt of proposals is *September 1, 1986.* Contributors will be notified by *November 1, 1986,* of the topic that best fits into the overall plan for organization of the volume. The final papers (6 to 8 double-spaced pages) will be due by the non-negotiable deadline of *February 1, 1987.* Send to: Dr. Muriel Vasconcellos, 1802 Corcoran Street, N.W., Washington, D.C. 20009.

Corporate Members

(AS OF MARCH 15, 1986)

ACCENTO, The Language Company
Accurapid Translations International, Inc.
AdEx Translations International, Inc.
AD-EX Translations International/USA
A E Inc.
Alice C. Grandoff Translating Service, Inc.
Amway Corporation
Bergen Language Institute
Boston Translation Company
CACI Language Center
Cosmopolitan Translation Bureau, Inc.
CRH & Associates
Data General Corporation, Translation Services Department
Dialogos International, Inc.
Euramerica Translations, Inc.
F.B.Morgan and Professors Interpreting
FLS, Inc.
Galaxy Systems, Inc.
Garden State Translations, Inc.
Globalink, L. P.
House of Tutor, Ltd.
Ibero-American Productions
Ingenieurbüro für technische und naturwissenschaftliche Übersetzungen
International Institute of Technology & Linguistics
JLS
Joyce M. Fernandez Translating
The Language Service, Inc.
Latin American Scholarly Services
Life Publishers International
Linguistic Systems, Inc.
Logos Corporation

Mellon Bank, Pittsburgh, PA
Pacific Basin Scribe Services
Polyglot Translations
Professional Translating Services
Ralph McElroy Company Inc.
Rennert Bilingual Translations
Rocky Mountain Translators
Scientific Communication Service
Sperry Corporation
Technical Translation International Ltd
The Toin Corporation
Translingua Associates
University Language Services, Inc.
Volkswagen of America
Weidner Communications Corporation
William L. Gray Enterprises, Inc.
Wychwood Press, Inc., Wychwood Language Services
Xerox Corporation

Institutional Members

(AS OF MARCH 15, 1986)

American Institute of Chemical Engineers
Asia Foreign Language Institute
Ball State University, Department of Foreign Languages
The Christian Science Publishing Society, Translation Department
Church of Jesus Christ of Latter-Day Saints, Translation Division
Eric Clearinghouse on Languages
Georgia State University, Department of Foreign Languages
Instituto Mexicano Norteamericano de Relaciones Culturales Valle, A.C.
Kearney State College, Department of Foreign Languages
Laurentian University, School of Translators and Interpreters
Mayo Clinic Language Department
Monterey Institute of International Studies
New York University, School of Continuing Education
Notre Dame College, Department of Modern Languages
Purdue University-Calumet, Foreign Languages and Literatures
Rose-Hulman Institute of Technology, Division of Humanities
Rutgers University, Department of Germanic Languages and Literatures
Seattle/King County Convention & Visitors Bureau
Stanford University, Department of German Studies
Stephens College, Department of Foreign Languages
Summer Institute of Linguistics, Translation Department
SUNY-Binghamton, Translation Research & Instruction Program
Travelers Aid-International Institute
University of Idaho, Library
University of Pittsburgh, Professional Translation Program
University of Surrey, Centre for Translation Studies
World Bank, Language Services Division
World Education Services, Inc.

American Translators Association, Officers and Board of Directors, 1986

Patricia E. Newman, President   Karl Kummer, President-Elect
Deanna L. Hammond, Secretary   Lloyd K. Vandersall, Treasurer
William I. Bertsche, Ralph Costa, Ted Crump, Henry Fischbach,
Kurt Gingold, Astrid Johanson, Marilyn Gaddis Rose, Grace Till-
inghast, Leslie Willson, René Deschamps (Canadian liaison)

Recipients of the Alexander Gode Medal

1964 Alexander Gode
     (deceased)
1965 Kurt Gingold
1966 Richard and Clara
     Winston (deceased)
1967 The National Translation
     Center
     (Austin, Texas, defunct)
1968 Pierre-François Caillé
     (deceased)
1969 Henry Fischbach
1970 Carl V. Bertsche
     (deceased)
1971 Lewis Bertrand (deceased)
1972 Lewis Galantière
     (deceased)

1973 Jean-Paul Vinay
1974 Eliot F. Beach
1975 Frederick Ungar
1977 Eugene Nida
1978 Royal L. Tinsley, Jr.
1980 Gregory Rabassa
1981 Georgetown University,
     Monterey Institute of
     International Studies,
     University Center at
     Binghamton (SUNY)
1983 Françoise Cestac
1984 Charles M. Stern
1985 Ludmilla Callaham
     Richard Ernst